William Carlos Williams was born in Rutherford, New Jersey, in 1883. He lived there most of his life, practising medicine as a pediatrician. While studying at the Pennsylvania Medical School he became a friend of Ezra Pound and H. Doolittle, and was deeply influenced by Imagism. This was reflected in his first books, *Poems* (1909) and *The Tempers* (1913). The limitations of Imagism soon led him to launch his own campaign to 'create somehow by intense, individual effort, a new – an American – poetic language'. In 1920 he wrote, 'I'll write whatever I damn please, whenever I damn please, and as I damn please . . .' He published *Al Que Quiere!* in 1917 and many other volumes of poetry followed. His later collections include *The Desert Music* (1954), *Journey to Love* (1955) and *Pictures from Brueghel* (1963), which won the Pulitzer Prize. *Patterson*, a long, structureless poem, appeared in five volumes between 1946–58. He wrote two volumes of essays, *The Great American Novel* (1923) and *Selected Essays* (1954); his collected plays, *Many Loves*; collections of stories, *The Knife of the Times* (1932), *Life Along the Passaic River* (1938), *Make Light of It* (1950) and *The Farmers' Daughters* (1961); and four novels, *A Voyage to Pagany* (1928), *White Mule* (1937), *In the Money* (1940) and *The Build-Up* (1952). He published an *Autobiography* (1951), *Selected Letters* (1957) and *Yes, Mrs. Williams* (1960), a memoir of his mother. William Carlos Williams died in 1963.

He was described by one critic as 'remarkably alert to the subtler life of the senses: how it feels to be a growing thing of any kind, or to come into birth; how the freshness of the morning or the feel of a particular moment in a particular season impresses itself upon us; what impact the people glimpsed in myriad transitory situations have upon us at the moment of the event. This alertness is intimately related to his faith in the power of art to reveal the meaning of experienced reality and even as he says, "to right all wrongs".'

WILLIAM CARLOS WILLIAMS
SELECTED POEMS

Edited with an introduction
by Charles Tomlinson

PENGUIN BOOKS

PENGUIN BOOKS

Published by the Penguin Group
Penguin Books Ltd, 27 Wrights Lane, London w8 5tz, England
Penguin Putnam Inc., 375 Hudson Street, New York, New York 10014, USA
Penguin Books Australia Ltd, Ringwood, Victoria, Australia
Penguin Books Canada Ltd, 10 Alcorn Avenue, Toronto, Ontario, Canada m4v 3b2
Penguin Books India (P) Ltd, 11, Community Centre, Panchsheel Park, New Delhi – 110 017, India
Penguin Books (NZ) Ltd, Private Bag 102902, NSMC, Auckland, New Zealand
Penguin Books (South Africa) (Pty) Ltd, 5 Watkins Street, Denver Ext 4, Johannesburg 2094, South Africa

Penguin Books Ltd, Registered Offices: Harmondsworth, Middlesex, England

This selection first published 1976
Reprinted in Penguin Classics 2000

I

The Acknowledgements on p. 10 constitute
an extension of this copyright page

Printed and bound in Great Britain by
Antony Rowe Ltd, Chippenham, Wiltshire
Set in Monotype Bembo

CONTENTS

CONTENTS

From COLLECTED POEMS 1921–1931 (1934)

From AN EARLY MARTYR (1935)

CONTENTS

CONTENTS

9

ACKNOWLEDGEMENTS

For permission to reprint poems in copyright acknow-
ledgement is made to the following:

Al Que Quiere! copyright © The Four Seas Company,
1917; *Sour Grapes* copyright © The Four Seas Company,
1921; *Spring and All* copyright © The Objectivist Press,
1934; *Collected Poems 1921–1931* copyright © The Objec-
tivist Press, 1934; *An Early Martyr* copyright © The
Alcestis Press, 1935; *Adam and Eve and the City* copyright
© Ronald Lane Latimer, 1936; *The Complete Collected
Poems 1906–1938* copyright © William Carlos Williams,
1938; *The Broken Span* copyright © William Carlos
Williams, 1941; *The Wedge* copyright © William Carlos
Williams, 1944; *The Clouds* copyright © William Carlos
Williams, 1948; *The Collected Later Poems* copyright ©
William Carlos Williams, 1950; *The Desert Music* copy-
right © William Carlos Williams, 1954; *Journey to Love*
copyright © William Carlos Williams, 1955; *Pictures
from Brueghel* copyright © William Carlos Williams,
1962; *Paterson* copyright © William Carlos Williams,
1958. Reprinted by permission of New Directions
Publishing Corporation.

INTRODUCTION

It was Ezra Pound, that indefatigable discoverer of talent, who
first seized on the essential elements in Williams's poetry. Intro-
ducing Williams's second, still tentative, volume, *The Tempers*, in
1913, Pound quoted one of Williams's similes where he speaks of
a thousand freshets:

> ... crowded
> Like peasants to a fair
> Clear skinned, wild from seclusion.

Pound has instinctively isolated here elements thoroughly charac-
teristic of this poet's entire venture – poetic energy imagined as the
rush of water; not so much Wordsworth's 'spontaneous over-
flow of powerful feelings', but feelings 'crowded', forcing and
yet constrained by their own earth-bound track; a certain rustic
uncouthness whose end is a celebration and which wears the stamp
of locality. 'The only universal', as Williams was to say later, 'is
the local as savages, artists and – to a lesser extent – peasants
know.'

The most interesting of Williams's early volumes, *Al Que
Quiere!*, appeared in 1917, the same year as T. S. Eliot's *Prufrock
and Other Observations*. Pound was there to salute the arrival of
both volumes and to differentiate them:

> Distinct and as different as possible from the orderly statements of
> an Eliot ... are the poems of Carlos Williams. If the sinuosities of
> Misses Moore and Loy are difficult to follow I do not know what is
> to be said for Mr Williams's ramifications and abruptnesses. I do not
> pretend to follow all of his volts, jerks, sulks, balks, outblurts and
> jump-overs; but for all this roughness there remains with me the
> conviction that there is nothing meaningless in his book, *Al que
> Quiere*, not a line ...

Perhaps Pound overstates the 'roughness' of Williams, but, in
pointing out the 'jerks, balks, outblurts and jump-overs', he has
arrived at one of the earliest and most accurate formulations of
what Williams's verse was about. Not only is 'locality' (a sticking

to New Jersey when Pound and Eliot had chosen European exile) the geographic source of Williams's poetry, but 'locality', seen as the jerks and outblurts of speech rendered on to the here and now of the page, is the source of his lineation. In the imaginative play of Williams's poems, where the attention is frequently turned upon outward things, the sound structure of the poems which embody that attention is an expression of strains, breath pauses, bodily constrictions and releases. Thus Williams's 'locality' begins with a somatic awareness, a physiological presence in time and space, and this in quite early poems. When he starts on his longest poem, *Paterson*, in the mid-forties, it is the remembrance of the act of walking through a given terrain which propels some of its best stretches, the gerund 'walking' itself used as a repeated motif and, at one point, checked against the descriptions of an article, 'Dynamic Posture', from *Journal of the American Medical Association*: 'The body is tilted slightly forward from the basic standing position and the weight thrown on the ball of the foot, while the other thigh is lifted and the leg and opposite arm are swung forward (fig. 6B) ...' A sentence from later on in this article (quoted by M. Weaver in his *William Carlos Williams, The American Background*) would doubtless have appealed to Williams in his identification of poet and walker: 'The good walker should be able to change pace, stop, start, turn, step up or down, twist or stoop, easily and quickly, without losing balance or rhythm ...' The Williams poem finds analogies for most of these movements.

The relation between subject and object appears in Williams in a series of images of physical strain – a poem from *Al Que Quiere!*, 'Spring Strains' (p. 29), feels out its own balks and resistances against those of the scene outside where the swift flight of two birds is challenged, as:

> the blinding and red-edged sun-blur –
> creeping energy, concentrated
> counterforce – welds sky, buds, trees,
> rivets them in one puckering hold!

At the close, the birds exert their own counterforce of speed and lightness, breaking out of the riveted landscape flung outward and up – disappearing suddenly!

– the poem imparting a verb-like force to its combined preposi-
tions, 'outward and up', and ending, as so often in Williams, on a
dangling clause that pulls the main clause towards incompletion
and assymetry.

This predilection for the open-ended and assymetrical leaves
Williams free to accept the suggestion of his surroundings with
their evidence of overlap and relativity –

> roof out of line with sides
> the yards cluttered
> with old chicken wire, ashes,
> furniture gone wrong;
> the fences and outhouses
> built of barrel-staves
> and parts of boxes . . .

Instead of wishing simply to reform the poor ('It's the anarchy of
poverty/delights me . . .'), he senses there is a point where the
imagination, partaking of this anarchy, could dance with it, could
'lift' it to an answering form, but a form fully responsive to the
waywardness and inconclusiveness of daily realities. The broken
fringes of the city in 'Morning' (p. 120) witness a sort of heroism
among 'diminished things', humorously absurd:

> And a church spire sketched on the sky,
> of sheet-metal and open beams, to resemble
> a church spire . . .

Williams hears in all this, and in the profusion of natural fact, a
kind of music – 'a vague melody/of harsh threads', as he says in
'Trees' (p. 30) where the tree which first catches his eye is
'crooked', 'bent . . . from straining / against the bitter horizontals
of / a north wind', the jump-overs at the line breaks enacting the
pressure of that straining. There is no romantic fusion of subject
and object possible in this nature poem: the voices of the trees may
be 'blent willingly / against the heaving contra-bass / of the dark'
but the contra-bass remains contra, the crooked tree warps itself
'passionately to one side' and the poem still presses forward as

Williams adds 'in [its] eagerness', the poem like the tree dissociating itself from a blent music for that 'melody / of harsh threads'. 'Bent' puns and rhymes eagerly against 'blent' in this piece.

When Williams in his turn paid tribute to Pound, he saw the poet – himself and Pound included – as seeking a language which 'will embody all the advantageous jumps, swiftnesses, colours, movements of the day . . .' He was praising the collage element in the poetry of Pound's *A Draft of XXX Cantos*, but the terms of his praise ignore those other elements of archaism and of the *musée imaginaire* that Williams distrusted in his friend. Both Pound and Eliot, or so Williams felt, had lost contact – it was a word whose meaning he was to go on exploring – with their American roots: they had sold out to Europe that American renaissance of which Pound himself had spoken, one which he had prophesied would 'overshadow the quattrocento'. It was an old story, for the trend of the American mind 'back to Europe' had grown in its appeal in nineteenth century America. Williams, who feels the pull himself in his first novel, *A Voyage to Pagany*, reflected towards the end of his life:

The novels of Henry James featured this seeking of Europe by the heiresses of America. He himself, for complex reasons . . . fled to the assurances of Victorian England. It was understandable, it was even admirable in him. He became a distinguished citizen in the republic of letters and a great artist. But he left another world behind. He abandoned it.

Williams's poetry and novels explore an America his two most powerful contemporaries also left behind, in the raw merging of American pastoral and urban squalor. He described his struggle to make articulate that world, in *Paterson*, as 'a reply to Greek and Latin with the bare hands'. Williams exaggerates, of course, and as he himself well knew his insistence on 'contact' and 'locality' needed for its completion an awareness that was also European – the kind of awareness he recognized immediately in the reproduction of a painting by Juan Gris, with its cubist sharpness, its almost fastidious handling of a world of broken forms. 'Contact' had been Whitman's word: 'I am mad for it to be in contact with me,' says Whitman of nature in *Song of Myself*. So is Williams. The difference lies in the *eruditus* of that *tactus eruditus* he speaks of in one poem. 'A fact with him', says Kenneth Burke, 'finds its justification in the trimness of the wording.' Whitman is a great poet, but he is never trim. Trimness was something Williams could recognize and applaud in Juan Gris's 'admirable simplicity and excellent design'.

When he speaks in the prose parts of *Spring and All* (1923) of Whitman, the company he puts him into is that of two great Europeans, Gris and Cézanne, announcing that 'Whitman's proposals are of the same piece with the modern trend toward imaginative understanding of life'. At this point, the imagination for Williams was identified with the cubist re-structuring of reality: modern poetry with its ellipses, its confrontation of disparates, its use of verbal collages – a device both Pound and Eliot had used – provided direct analogies. In *Spring and All*, after a rapid transition from Gris, Cézanne and Whitman to Shakespeare, Williams tells us of the last named: 'He holds no mirror up to nature but with his imagination rivals nature's composition with his own.' Shakespeare, too, could be made to belong to the moment of cubism. This seems a far cry from 'a reply to Greek and Latin with the bare hands'.

Kenneth Rexroth, in an excellent and too little known essay, 'The Influence of French Poetry on American' (reprinted in the Penguin critical anthology, *William Carlos Williams*, edited by the present writer) has commented on Williams's cubist allegiances and expresses the relation between these and Williams's stress on localism – 'place' and 'contact' – with great perspicacity:

Williams could be said to belong in the Cubist tradition – Imagism, Objectivism, the dissociation and rearrangement of the elements of concrete reality, rather than rhetoric or free association. But where Reverdy, Apollinaire, Salmon, Cendrars, Cocteau and Jacob are all urban, even megalopolitan, poets of that Paris which is the international market of objects of *vertu*, vice, and art, Williams has confined himself in single strictness to the life before his eyes – the life of a physician in a small town twenty miles from New York. In so doing, his localism has become international and timeless. His long quest for a completely defenseless simplicity of personal speech produces an idiom identical with that which is the end product of centuries of polish, refinement, tradition and revolution.

On the face of it, the inheritance Williams brings to cubism seems to be very close in spirit not only to Whitman but also to Emerson and Thoreau. If 'contact' is re-explored, so is Emerson's attachment to the vernacular: 'the speech of Polish mothers' was where Williams insisted he got his English from. 'Colleges and books only copy the language which the field and work-yard made,' said Emerson. Williams's famous 'flatness' comes not from the field, but from the urban 'work-yard' of New Jersey. As Hugh Kenner writes of Williams's characteristic diction: 'That words set in Jersey speech rhythms mean less but mean it with greater finality, is Williams's great technical perception.'

Emerson seems to have prepared the ground for Williams's other war-cry, 'No ideas but in things' with his 'Ask the fact for the form'. Thoreau sounds yet closer with: 'The roots of letters are things.' Again Emerson tells over things – 'The meal in the firkin; the milk in the pan; the ballad in the street; the news of the boat . . .' – in the shape of a list very like Williams's 'rigmaroles', as he calls his poems. 'Bare lists of words,' says Emerson, 'are found suggestive to an imaginative mind.' When Williams, long after Emerson and after Whitman's application of this, constructed 'list' poems, he came in for suspicion, as in the interview which he prints as part of *Paterson 5* and in which, defending what amounts to a grocery list that forms the jagged pattern of one of his later poems, he concludes: 'Anything is good material for poetry. Anything. I've said it time and time again.'

Paterson 5 came out in 1958. Years before, Williams had formulated his kind of poem made out of anything and with a jagged pattern, in the 1920 preface to *Kora in Hell*, when he wrote that a poem is 'tough by no quality it borrows from a logical recital of events nor from the events themselves but solely from the attenuated power which draws perhaps many broken things into a dance by giving them thus a full being'. He was often to return to the idea of poem as dance. If, as with Emerson, Williams seems to 'ask the fact for the form', the form, once it comes, is free of the fact, is a *dance above* the fact. After *Kora in Hell* he had another

16

shot at the formula in the prose of *Spring and All*, where he con-
cludes of John of Gaunt's speech in *Richard II* that 'his words are
related not to their sense as objects adherent to his son's welfare or
otherwise, but as a dance over the body of his condition accurately
accompanying it'.

J. Hillis Miller in his book *Poets of Reality* has argued that
Williams marks an historic moment for modern poetry in that his
work sees the disappearance of all dualism. If it is not from dualism
it is yet from a duality that much of the interest of his work arises:
the words 'accurately accompany' a perception of the forms of
reality, they dance over or with these forms, but it is the gap be-
tween words and forms that gives poetry its chance to exist and to
go on existing. Williams's most truncated and Zen-like expression
of this fact comes in the tiny

> so much depends
> upon
>
> a red wheel
> barrow
>
> glazed with rain
> water
>
> beside the white
> chickens

What depends on the red wheelbarrow for Williams is the fact
that its presence can be rendered over into words, that the per-
ception can be slowed down and meditated on by regulating, line
by line, the gradual appearance of these words. The imagination
'accurately accompanies' the wheelbarrow, or whatever facets
of reality attract Williams, by not permitting too ready and
emotional a fusion with them. When things go badly the imagina-
tion retreats into a subjective anguish –

> to an empty, windswept place
> without sun, stars or moon
> but a peculiar light as of thought

17

> that spins a dark fire –
> whirling upon itself . . .   ('These', p. 119)

But when the dance with facts suffices, syntax, the forms of grammar, puns, the ambiguous pull between words unpunctuated or divided by line-endings, these all contribute to – accompany – the richness of a reality one can never completely fuse with, but which affords a resistance whereby the I can know itself.

One has in Williams's best verse a vivid sense of what Olson calls 'the elements and minims of language', down to the syllabic components or 'the diphthong/ae' ('To Have Done Nothing' p. 47). It is this drama of elements, played across the ends of frequently short lines, which gives to Williams's 'free verse' its cohesiveness, and intensifies what Olson calls

> The contingent motion of
>   each line as it
>   moves with – or against –
>   the whole – working
>   particularly out of its immediacy.

Williams insisted that he did not write free verse, of course. As early as 1913 he was saying: 'I do not believe in *vers libre*, this contradiction in terms. Either the motion continues or it does not continue, either there is rhythm or no rhythm.' In the same essay ('Speech Rhythm', quoted by Weaver, pp. 82–3), Williams writes that, in an Odyssey, 'rightly considered', 'no part in its excellence but partakes of the essential nature of the whole':

This is the conception of the action that I want. In the other direction, inward: Imagination creates an image, point by point, piece by piece, segment by segment – into a whole, living. But each part as it plays into its neighbour, each segment into its neighbour segment and every part into every other, causing the whole – exists naturally in rhythm, and as there are waves there are tides and as there are ridges in the sand there are bars after bars . . .

This intuitive conception of the kind of poetic writing he sought gets closer to essentials than Williams's later and self-defeating attempts to define the 'variable foot', that 'relative measure' which ends by being what Williams said *vers libre* was, a contradiction in terms. It is 'the contingent motion of / each line' and what Robert Creeley has referred to as the 'contentual emphases' of each line that give life to Williams's verse, rather than any prosodic notion of feet. These emphases are brought to bear most consistently perhaps in relatively short poems. *Paterson* has its incidental finenesses, but there are stretches when one feels, as in others of the more lengthy pieces, that the dance has broken down. At the same time, some of the longer poems, unachieved as a whole, frequently contain passages of great brilliance. Yvor Winters is reminded by Williams of the brevity of a Herrick, which is to narrow Williams's range somewhat unduly; after all, he is capable of the extended range of poems like 'The Crimson Cyclamen' and 'Elena'. The shorter poems are certainly more proof against that meditative self-regard which elsewhere often makes for sentimental proliferation. Even a poem initially as fine as 'The Orchestra' (p. 181) runs aground on the most banal professions of innocence.

Williams may not have been capable of the unity of *The Waste Land*, but, as Octavio Paz insists, introducing his translations of Williams in *Veinte Poemas*, 'The greatness of a poet is not to be measured by the scale but by the intensity and the perfection of his works. Also by his vivacity. Williams is the author of the most *vivid* poems of modern American poetry.' And the vivacity arises, one might add, from the unexpectedness of Williams's apparently wayward forms. How, for example, in 'Raindrops on a Briar' (p. 152), did one get from the opening statement to those water-drops 'ranged upon the arching stems / irregularly as an accompaniment', and yet wasn't that devious track the poem's most exact way of saying what it had to and by a superb use of form?

Williams's attitude to form rather resembles his attitude to friendship, which should be, he says, 'dangerous – uncertain – made of many questionable crossties, I think, that might fail it. But while they last, give it a good cellular structure – paths, private connections between the members – full of versatility.' This passage comes from Williams's *Autobiography* – Chapter 49, 'Friendship'. In Chapter 50, 'Projective Verse', it is silently transfigured into an ideal of artistic form, and this ideal is seen as part and parcel of Williams's conception of locality. Chapter 50 is, in many ways, pivotal to the book, for, in using Charles Olson's conception of 'composition by field', Williams does so – and very tactfully – against an implied background of why his forms were not readily understood in his own country or ours, why 'The Criterion had no place for me', why Eliot's *The Waste Land* had seemed to him 'the great catastrophe to our letters . . . Eliot had turned his back on the possibility of reviving my world'. That world seemed to Williams to receive its recognition in Olson's 'Projective Verse' essay, with its preference for an explorative, syllable-based verse and its invitation 'to step back here to this place of the elements and minims of language . . . to engage speech where it is least careless – and least logical'. In Chapter 50 Williams juxtaposes 'this place of elements' with an *actual* place – and the leap is beautifully justified in the chapter as a whole – with the painter Charles Sheeler taking over a small stone house on a ravaged New York estate and making of it 'a cell, a seed of intelligence and feeling security'. 'The poem,' says Williams, 'is our objective, the secret at the heart of the matter – as Sheeler's small house, re-organised, is the heart of the gone estate of the Lowes . . .' Sheeler and his Russian wife and what they do with the local conditions are vibrant with meaning for Williams as a poet, and the form of the chapter lays bare that meaning: 'It is ourselves we organise in this way not against the past or for the future or even for survival but for integrity of understanding to insure persistence, to give the mind its stay.' Coming, as it does, in the last lap of the book, this makes a fine conscious formulation for the many years of groping with the potentials of language and it balances foursquare in the American locality a mind that had gone back to it armed – despite Williams's frequent protests – by Europe. The figures who stand out in those autobiographical pages are Joyce and Brancusi as well as Sheeler and Demuth: Paris counterpoints Rutherford and New York.

Of all the American modernists Williams was the most tardy in receiving recognition. His writing lifetime was dominated by the literary criteria of T. S. Eliot and the New Criticism, in neither of whose terminology was there a place for the kind of thing Williams was concerned with doing. Parker Tyler imagines Williams explaining why T. S. Eliot's theory of the objective correlative was not for him and where its shortcomings lay: 'My theory of poetry was that it arises from immediate environment, and in the case of *my* environment, America, the poetic formulas for familiar (or 'objective correlative') emotions did not exist. Why not? Because the emotions themselves, and the very imagery of their implicit situations, were elusive and unformed.'

To name what possessed no name, to avoid surrendering oneself 'into the inverted cone of waning energy ... [and] fly off at last into nonentity, general deracinate conclusions', were the tasks that Williams had recognized early on – earlier, in fact, than the 1913 essay, 'Speech Rhythm', quoted above. *How* early one realizes in his accounts of his undergraduate poem (which he burned) about the prince who is abducted and taken to an unknown country – Williams's inarticulate America – to wake confronted by all the problems of language and cultural identity that Williams himself was to face: 'No one was there to inform him of his whereabouts and when he did begin to encounter passers-by, they didn't even understand, let alone speak his language. He could recall nothing of the past ... So he went on, homeward or seeking a home that was his own, all this through a "foreign" country whose language was barbarous.'

This myth would seem to lend itself to a long psychic alienation. But one sees Williams breaking through by meeting the demands of day-to-day existence, never too involved in himself to feel the ballast of place, people and things. The source of his resilience recalls his hero, the Jesuit Père Rasles, among the Indians, of *In the American Grain*: 'This is a moral source not reckoned with, peculiarly sensitive and daring in its close embrace of native things ... For everything his fine sense, blossoming, thriving, opening, reviving – not shutting out – was tuned. He speaks of his struggles with their language, its peculiar beauties, "je ne sais quoi d'énergique", he cited its tempo, the form of its genius with gusto, with admiration, with generosity.'

The myth of the prince and the necessity of a counter-statement to it underlie Williams's work. In his *Autobiography*, the counter-statement reappears in the final pages when he drives out to look at the site of the poem, *Paterson*: 'The Falls let out a roar as it crashed upon the rocks at its base. In the imagination this roar is a speech or a voice, a speech in particular; it is the poem itself that is the answer.'

A NOTE ON THIS SELECTION

The ordinary reader, coming to Williams with a desire to form some chronological sense of the poet's development, is ill-served by the book with which he will most probably begin, *The Collected Earlier Poems*. Opening it, he finds himself confronted by *The Wanderer, A Rococo Study*. This long poem is a later publication than the collection, *The Tempers*, which is reprinted after it. But this is a mild enough reversal of chronology compared with what follows: despite a snippet from *Al Que Quiere!* (1917) we suddenly find ourselves in a sequence, 'Della Primavera Trasportata Al Morale', which first appeared in 1934. On page 83 *An Early Martyr* appears, a volume of 1935. Thirty or more pages later we are brought back to the rest of *Al Que Quiere! Spring and All*, which predates *An Early Martyr* by twelve years, comes on the scene more than fifty pages further on. The puzzling transpositions of individual poems in both *The Collected Earlier Poems* and *The Collected Later Poems* help to confound matters a little more. Both of these collections are without much in the way of dates to place individual volumes. What I have attempted to do is to re-sort the strayed poems into the volume where they first appeared. Although only the second version of 'The Locust Tree in Flower' (p. 89) appeared in *An Early Martyr*, I have, however, printed the first version beside it. I have reprinted extracts from Williams's long poem, *Paterson*, all together (the dates of publication of the various books of this are given) rather than chop it up between volumes of shorter poems which punctuated its appearance. The poem, 'Tribute to the Painters', first appears in *Journey to Love* (1955): Williams reprinted a rather insensitively cut version of this in *Paterson*, Book 5 (1958). I have chosen the earlier form of it.

AL QUE QUIERE!
[1917]

PASTORAL *? link with green ?*

Statement {
When I was younger
it was plain to me
I must make something of myself.
Older now
I walk back streets
admiring the houses
of the very poor: *resentment*
roof out of line with sides
the yards cluttered
with old chicken wire, ashes,
furniture gone wrong;
the fences and outhouses
built of barrel-staves
and parts of boxes, all,
if I am fortunate,
smeared a bluish green
that properly weathered
pleases me best
of all colors.

No one
will believe this
of vast import to the nation.)

TRACT

I will teach you my townspeople
how to perform a funeral
for you have it over a troop
of artists –
unless one should scour the world –
you have the ground sense necessary.

25

See! the hearse leads.
I begin with a design for a hearse.
For Christ's sake not black –
nor white either – and not polished!
Let it be weathered – like a farm wagon –
with gilt wheels (this could be
applied fresh at small expense)
or no wheels at all:
a rough dray to drag over the ground.

Knock the glass out!
My God – glass, my townspeople!
For what purpose? Is it for the dead
to look out or for us to see
how well he is housed or to see
the flowers or the lack of them –
or what?
To keep the rain and snow from him?
He will have a heavier rain soon:
pebbles and dirt and what not.
Let there be no glass –
and no upholstery, phew!
and no little brass rollers
and small easy wheels on the bottom –
my townspeople what are you thinking of?
A rough plain hearse then
with gilt wheels and no top at all.
On this the coffin lies
by its own weight.

                    No wreaths please –
especially no hot house flowers.
Some common memento is better,
something he prized and is known by:
his old clothes – a few books perhaps –
God knows what! You realize
how we are about these things

26

my townspeople –
something will be found – anything
even flowers if he had come to that.
So much for the hearse.

For heaven's sake though see to the driver!
Take off the silk hat! In fact
that's no place at all for him –
up there unceremoniously
dragging our friend out to his own dignity!
Bring him down – bring him down!
Low and inconspicuous! I'd not have him ride
on the wagon at all – damn him –
the undertaker's understrapper!
Let him hold the reins
and walk at the side
and inconspicuously too!

Then briefly as to yourselves:
Walk behind – as they do in France,
seventh class, or if you ride
Hell take curtains! Go with some show
of inconvenience; sit openly –
to the weather as to grief.
Or do you think you can shut grief in?
What – from us? We who have perhaps
nothing to lose? Share with us
share with us – it will be money
in your pockets.
                              Go now
I think you are ready.

APOLOGY

Why do I write today?

The beauty of
the terrible faces
of our nonentities
stirs me to it:

colored women
day workers –
old and experienced –
returning home at dusk
in cast off clothing
faces like
old Florentine oak.
Also

the set pieces
of your faces stir me –
leading citizens –
but not
in the same way.

equality?
anti slavery?

PASTORAL

The little sparrows
hop ingenuously
about the pavement
quarreling
with sharp voices
over those things
that interest them.
But we who are wiser

shut ourselves in
on either hand
and no one knows
whether we think good
or evil.

Meanwhile,
the old man who goes about
gathering dog-lime
walks in the gutter
without looking up
and his tread
is more majestic than
that of the Episcopal minister
approaching the pulpit
of a Sunday.
These things
astonish me beyond words.

EL HOMBRE

It's a strange courage
you give me ancient star:

Shine alone in the sunrise
toward which you lend no part!

SPRING STRAINS

In a tissue-thin monotone of blue-grey buds
crowded erect with desire against the sky
tense blue-grey twigs
slenderly anchoring them down, drawing
them in –

two blue-grey birds chasing
a third struggle in circles, angles,
swift convergings to a point that bursts
instantly!

Vibrant bowing limbs
pull downward, sucking in the sky
that bulges from behind, plastering itself
against them in packed rifts, rock blue
and dirty orange!

But –

(Hold hard, rigid jointed trees!)
the blinding and red-edged sun-blur –
creeping energy, concentrated
counterforce – welds sky, buds, trees,
rivets them in one puckering hold!
Sticks through! Pulls the whole
counter-pulling mass upward, to the right
locks even the opaque, not yet defined
ground in a terrific drag that is
loosening the very tap-roots!

On a tissue-thin monotone of blue-grey buds
two blue-grey birds, chasing a third,
at full cry! Now they are
flung outward and up – disappearing suddenly!

TREES

Crooked, black tree
on your little grey-black hillock,
ridiculously raised one step toward
the infinite summits of the night:
even you the few grey stars
draw upward into a vague melody
of harsh threads.

30

Bent as you are from straining
against the bitter horizontals of
a north wind, – there below you
how easily the long yellow notes
of poplars flow upward in a descending
scale, each note secure in its own
posture – singularly woven.

All voices are blent willingly
against the heaving contra-bass
of the dark but you alone
warp yourself passionately to one side
in your eagerness.

TO A SOLITARY DISCIPLE

Rather notice, mon cher,
that the moon is
tilted above
the point of the steeple
than that its color
is shell-pink.

Rather observe
that it is early morning
than that the sky
is smooth
as a turquoise.

Rather grasp
how the dark
converging lines
of the steeple
meet at the pinnacle –
perceive how
its little ornament
tries to stop them –

See how it fails!
See how the converging lines
of the hexagonal spire
escape upward –
receding, dividing!
– sepals
that guard and contain
the flower!

Observe
how motionless
the eaten moon
lies in the protecting lines.
It is true:
in the light colors
of morning

brown-stone and slate
shine orange and dark blue.

But observe
the oppressive weight
of the squat edifice!
Observe
the jasmine lightness
of the moon.

DEDICATION FOR A PLOT OF GROUND

This plot of ground
facing the waters of this inlet
is dedicated to the living presence of
Emily Dickinson Wellcome
who was born in England, married,
lost her husband and with
her five year old son
sailed for New York in a two-master,
was driven to the Azores;

ran adrift on Fire Island shoal,
met her second husband
in a Brooklyn boarding house,
went with him to Puerto Rico
bore three more children, lost
her second husband, lived hard
for eight years in St Thomas,
Puerto Rico, San Domingo, followed
the oldest son to New York,
lost her daughter, lost her 'baby',
seized the two boys of
the oldest son by the second marriage
mothered them – they being
motherless – fought for them
against the other grandmother
and the aunts, brought them here
summer after summer, defended
herself here against thieves,
storms, sun, fire,
against flies, against girls
that came smelling about, against
drought, against weeds, storm-tides,
neighbors, weasels that stole her chickens,
against the weakness of her own hands,
against the growing strength of
the boys, against wind, against
the stones, against trespassers,
against rents, against her own mind.

She grubbed this earth with her own hands,
domineered over this grass plot,
blackguarded her oldest son
into buying it, lived here fifteen years,
attained a final loneliness and –

If you can bring nothing to this place
but your carcass, keep out.

SOUR GRAPES
[1921]

OVERTURE TO A DANCE OF LOCOMOTIVES

Men with picked voices chant the names
of cities in a huge gallery: promises
that pull through descending stairways
to a deep rumbling.

                  The rubbing feet
of those coming to be carried quicken a
grey pavement into soft light that rocks
to and fro, under the domed ceiling,
across and across from pale
earthcolored walls of bare limestone.

Covertly the hands of a great clock
go round and round! Were they to
move quickly and at once the whole
secret would be out and the shuffling
of all ants be done forever.

A leaning pyramid of sunlight, narrowing
out at a high window, moves by the clock;
discordant hands straining out from
a center: inevitable postures infinitely
repeated –

two – twofour – twoeight!

Porters in red hats run on narrow platforms.

This way ma'am!
                  – important not to take
the wrong train!

                            Lights from the concrete
ceiling hang crooked but –
                              Poised horizontal
on glittering parallels the dingy cylinders
packed with a warm glow – inviting entry –
pull against the hour. But brakes can
hold a fixed posture till –
                              The whistle!

Not twoeight. Not twofour. Two!

Gliding windows. Colored cooks sweating
in a small kitchen. Taillights –
In time: twofour!
In time: twoeight!

– rivers are tunneled: trestles
cross oozy swampland: wheels repeating
the same gesture remain relatively
stationary: rails forever parallel
return on themselves infinitely.
                      The dance is sure.

TO WAKEN AN OLD LADY

          Old age is
          a flight of small
          cheeping birds
          skimming
          bare trees
          above a snow glaze.
          Gaining and failing
          they are buffeted
          by a dark wind –
          But what?
          On harsh weedstalks

the flock has rested,
the snow
is covered with broken
seedhusks
and the wind tempered
by a shrill
piping of plenty.

ARRIVAL

And yet one arrives somehow,
finds himself loosening the hooks of
her dress
in a strange bedroom —
feels the autumn
dropping its silk and linen leaves
about her ankles.
The tawdry veined body emerges
twisted upon itself
like a winter wind ...!

THE WIDOW'S LAMENT IN SPRINGTIME

Sorrow is my own yard
where the new grass
flames as it has flamed
often before but not
with the cold fire
that closes round me this year.
Thirtyfive years
I lived with my husband.
The plumtree is white today
with masses of flowers.
Masses of flowers
load the cherry branches

and color some bushes
yellow and some red
but the grief in my heart
is stronger than they
for though they were my joy
formerly, today I notice them
and turn away forgetting.
Today my son told me
that in the meadows,
at the edge of the heavy woods
in the distance, he saw
trees of white flowers.
I feel that I would like
to go there
and fall into those flowers
and sink into the marsh near them.

BLUEFLAGS

I stopped the car
to let the children down
where the streets end
in the sun
at the marsh edge
and the reeds begin
and there are small houses
facing the reeds
and the blue mist
in the distance
with grapevine trellises
with grape clusters
small as strawberries
on the vines
and ditches
running springwater
that continue the gutters

with willows over them.
The reeds begin
like water at a shore
their pointed petals waving
dark green and light.
But blueflags are blossoming
in the reeds
which the children pluck
chattering in the reeds
high over their heads
which they part
with bare arms to appear
with fists of flowers
till in the air
there comes the smell
of calamus
from wet, gummy stalks.

THE LONELY STREET

School is over. It is too hot
to walk at ease. At ease
in light frocks they walk the streets
to while the time away.
They have grown tall. They hold
pink flames in their right hands.
In white from head to foot,
with sidelong, idle look –
in yellow, floating stuff,
black sash and stockings –
touching their avid mouths
with pink sugar on a stick –
like a carnation each holds in her hand –
they mount the lonely street.

THE GREAT FIGURE

Among the rain
and lights
I saw the figure 5
in gold
on a red
firetruck
moving
tense
unheeded
to gong clangs
siren howls
and wheels rumbling
through the dark city.

can't read fast.

slowly opens up.

42

SPRING AND ALL
[1923]

SPRING AND ALL

By the road to the contagious hospital
under the surge of the blue
mottled clouds driven from the
northeast – a cold wind. Beyond, the
waste of broad, muddy fields
brown with dried weeds, standing and fallen

patches of standing water
the scattering of tall trees

All along the road the reddish
purplish, forked, upstanding, twiggy
stuff of bushes and small trees
with dead, brown leaves under them
leafless vines –

Lifeless in appearance, sluggish
dazed spring approaches –

They enter the new world naked,
cold, uncertain of all
save that they enter. All about them
the cold, familiar wind –

Now the grass, tomorrow
the stiff curl of wildcarrot leaf
One by one objects are defined –
It quickens: clarity, outline of leaf

But now the stark dignity of
entrance – Still, the profound change
has come upon them: rooted, they
grip down and begin to awaken

THE POT OF FLOWERS

Pink confused with white
flowers and flowers reversed
take and spill the shaded flame
darting it back
into the lamp's horn

petals aslant darkened with mauve

red where in whorls
petal lays its glow upon petal
round flamegreen throats

petals radiant with transpiercing light
contending
        above
the leaves
reaching up their modest green
from the pot's rim

and there, wholly dark, the pot
gay with rough moss.

THE FARMER

The farmer in deep thought
is pacing through the rain
among his blank fields, with
hands in pockets,
in his head
the harvest already planted.
A cold wind ruffles the water
among the browned weeds.
On all sides

the world rolls coldly away:
black orchards
darkened by the March clouds –
leaving room for thought.
Down past the brushwood
bristling by
the rainsluiced wagonroad
looms the artist figure of
the farmer – composing
– antagonist

TO HAVE DONE NOTHING

No that is not it
nothing that I have done
nothing
I have done

is made up of
nothing
and the diphthong

ae

together with
the first person
singular
indicative

of the auxiliary
verb
to have

everything
I have done
is the same

47

if to do
is capable
of an
infinity of
combinations

involving the
moral
physical
and religious

codes

for everything
and nothing
are synonymous
when

energy *in vacuo*
has the power
of confusion

which only to
have done nothing
can make
perfect

THE ROSE

The rose is obsolete
but each petal ends in
an edge, the double facet
cementing the grooved
columns of air – The edge
cuts without cutting
meets – nothing – renews
itself in metal or porcelain –

whither? It ends –

But if it ends
the start is begun
so that to engage roses
becomes a geometry –

Sharper, neater, more cutting
figured in majolica –
the broken plate
glazed with a rose

Somewhere the sense
makes copper roses
steel roses –

The rose carried weight of love
but love is at an end – of roses
It is at the edge of the
petal that love waits

Crisp, worked to defeat
laboredness – fragile
plucked, moist, half-raised
cold, precise, touching

What

The place between the petal's
edge and the

From the petal's edge a line starts
that being of steel
infinitely fine, infinitely
rigid penetrates
the Milky Way
without contact – lifting

49

from it – neither hanging
nor pushing –

The fragility of the flower
unbruised
penetrates space.

AT THE FAUCET OF JUNE

The sunlight in a
yellow plaque upon the
varnished floor

is full of a song
inflated to
fifty pounds pressure

at the faucet of
June that rings
the triangle of the air

pulling at the
anemones in
Persephone's cow pasture –

When from among
the steel rocks leaps
J.P.M.

who enjoyed
extraordinary privileges
among virginity

to solve the core
of whirling flywheels
by cutting

the Gordian knot
with a Veronese or
perhaps a Rubens –

whose cars are about
the finest on
the market today –

And so it comes
to motor cars –
which is the son

leaving off the g
of sunlight and grass –
Impossible

to say, impossible
to underestimate –
wind, earthquakes in

Manchuria, a
partridge
from dry leaves.

THE EYEGLASSES

The universality of things
draws me toward the candy
with melon flowers that open

about the edge of refuse
proclaiming without accent
the quality of the farmer's

shoulders and his daughter's
accidental skin, so sweet
with clover and the small

yellow cinquefoil in the
parched places. It is
this that engages the favorable

distortion of eyeglasses
that see everything and remain
related to mathematics –

in the most practical frame of
brown celluloid made to
represent tortoiseshell –

A letter from the man who
wants to start a new magazine
made of linen

and he owns a typewriter –
July 1, 1922
All this is for eyeglasses

to discover. But
they lie there with the gold
earpieces folded down

tranquilly Titicaca –

THE RIGHT OF WAY

In passing with my mind
on nothing in the world

but the right of way
I enjoy on the road by

virtue of the law –
I saw

an elderly man who
smiled and looked away

to the north past a house –
a woman in blue

who was laughing and
leaning forward to look up

into the man's half
averted face

and a boy of eight who was
looking at the middle of

the man's belly
at a watchchain –

The supreme importance
of this nameless spectacle

sped me by them
without a word –

Why bother where I went?
for I went spinning on the

four wheels of my car
along the wet road until

I saw a girl with one leg
over the rail of a balcony

DEATH THE BARBER

Of death
the barber
the barber
talked to me

cutting my
life with
sleep to trim
my hair –

It's just
a moment
he said, we die
every night –

And of
the newest
ways to grow
hair on

bald death –
I told him
of the quartz
lamp

and of old men
with third
sets of teeth
to the cue

of an old man
who said
at the door –
Sunshine today!

for which
death shaves
him twice
a week

TO ELSIE

The pure products of America
go crazy –
mountain folk from Kentucky

or the ribbed north end of
Jersey
with its isolate lakes and

valleys, its deaf-mutes, thieves
old names
and promiscuity between

devil-may-care men who have taken
to railroading
out of sheer lust of adventure –

and young slatterns, bathed
in filth
from Monday to Saturday

to be tricked out that night
with gauds
from imaginations which have no

peasant traditions to give them
character
but flutter and flaunt

sheer rags – succumbing without
emotion
save numbed terror

under some hedge of choke-cherry
or viburnum –
which they cannot express –

Unless it be that marriage
perhaps
with a dash of Indian blood

will throw up a girl so desolate
so hemmed round
with disease or murder

that she'll be rescued by an
agent –
reared by the state and

sent out at fifteen to work in
some hard-pressed
house in the suburbs –

some doctor's family, some Elsie –
voluptuous water
expressing with broken

brain the truth about us –
her great
ungainly hips and flopping breasts

addressed to cheap
jewelry
and rich young men with fine eyes

as if the earth under our feet
were
an excrement of some sky

and we degraded prisoners
destined
to hunger until we eat filth

while the imagination strains
after deer
going by fields of goldenrod in

the stifling heat of September
Somehow
it seems to destroy us

It is only in isolate flecks that
something
is given off

No one
to witness
and adjust, no one to drive the car

THE RED WHEELBARROW

so much depends
upon

a red wheel
barrow

glazed with rain
water

beside the white
chickens.

Epiphany

AT THE BALL GAME

The crowd at the ball game
is moved uniformly

by a spirit of uselessness
which delights them –

all the exciting detail
of the chase

and the escape, the error
the flash of genius –

all to no end save beauty
the eternal –

So in detail they, the crowd,
are beautiful

for this
to be warned against

saluted and defied –
It is alive, venomous

it smiles grimly
its words cut –

The flashy female with her
mother, gets it –

The Jew gets it straight – it
is deadly, terrifying –

It is the Inquisition, the
Revolution

It is beauty itself
that lives

day by day in them
idly –

This is
the power of their faces

It is summer, it is the solstice
the crowd is

cheering, the crowd is laughing
in detail

permanently, seriously
without thought

COLLECTED POEMS
1921–1931

[1934]

YOUNG SYCAMORE

I must tell you
this young tree
whose round and firm trunk
between the wet

pavement and the gutter
(where water
is trickling) rises
bodily

into the air with
one undulant
thrust half its height –
and then

dividing and waning
sending out
young branches on
all sides –

hung with cocoons
it thins
till nothing is left of it
but two

eccentric knotted
twigs
bending forward
hornlike at the top

IT IS A LIVING CORAL

a trouble

archaically fettered
to produce

E Pluribus Unum an
island

in the sea a Capitol
surmounted

by Armed Liberty –
painting

sculpture straddled by
a dome

eight million pounds
in weight

iron plates constructed
to expand

and contract with
variations

of temperature
the folding

and unfolding of a lily.
And Congress

authorized and the
Commission

was entrusted was
entrusted!

a sculptured group
Mars

in Roman mail placing
a wreath

of laurel on the brow
of Washington

Commerce Minerva
Thomas

Jefferson John Hancock
at

the table Mrs Motte
presenting

Indian burning arrows
to Generals

Marion and Lee to fire
her mansion

and dislodge the British –
this scaleless

jumble is superb

and accurate in its
expression

of the thing they
would destroy –

Baptism of Poca-
hontas

with a little card
hanging

under it to tell
the persons

in the picture.

It climbs

it runs, it is Geo.
Shoup

of Idaho it wears
a beard

it fetches naked
Indian

women from a river
Trumbull

Varnum Henderson
Frances

Willard's corset is
absurd –

Banks White Columbus
stretched

in bed men felling trees

The Hon. Michael
C. Kerr

onetime Speaker of
the House

of Representatives
Perry

in a rowboat on Lake
Erie

changing ships the
dead

among the wreckage
sickly green

THE SUN BATHERS

A tramp thawing out
on a doorstep
against an east wall
Nov. 1, 1933:

a young man begrimed
and in an old
army coat
wriggling and scratching

while a fat negress
in a yellow house-window
nearby
leans out and yawns

into the fine weather

THE COD HEAD

Miscellaneous weed
strands, stems, debris –
firmament

to fishes –
where the yellow feet
of gulls dabble

oars whip
ships churn to bubbles –
at night wildly

agitate phosphores-
cent midges – but by day
flaccid

moons in whose
discs sometimes a red cross
lives – four

fathom – the bottom skids
a mottle of green
sands backward –

amorphous waver-
ing rocks – three fathom
the vitreous

body through which –
small scudding fish deep
down – and

now a lulling lift
and fall –
red stars – a severed cod –

head between two
green stones – lifting
falling

NEW ENGLAND*

is a condition –
of bedrooms whose electricity

is brickish or made into
T beams – They dangle them

on wire cables to the tops
of Woolworth buildings

five and ten cents worth –
There they have bolted them

into place at masculine risk –
Or a boy with a rose under

the lintel of his cap
standing to have his picture

taken on the butt of a girder
with the city a mile down –

captured, lonely cock atop
iron girders wears rosepetal

smile – a thought of Indians
on chestnut branches

to end 'walking on the air'

* Originally called 'Downtown'.

POEM

As the cat
climbed over
the top of

the jamcloset
first the right
forefoot

carefully
then the hind
stepped down

into the pit of
the empty
flowerpot

ON GAY WALLPAPER

The green-blue ground
is ruled with silver lines
to say the sun is shining

And on this moral sea
of grass or dreams lie flowers
or baskets of desires

Heaven knows what they are
between cerulean shapes
laid regularly round

Mat roses and tridentate
leaves of gold
threes, threes and threes

Three roses and three stems
the basket floating
standing in the horns of blue

Repeated to the ceiling
to the windows
where the day

Blows in
the scalloped curtains to
the sound of rain

NANTUCKET

Flowers through the window
lavender and yellow

changed by white curtains –
Smell of cleanliness –

Sunshine of late afternoon –
On the glass tray

a glass pitcher, the tumbler
turned down, by which

a key is lying – And the
immaculate white bed

THE ATTIC WHICH IS DESIRE

the unused tent
of

bare beams
beyond which

71

directly wait
the night

and day –
Here

from the street
by

```
*  *  *
*  S  *
*  O  *
*  D  *
*  A  *
*  *  *
```

ringed with
running lights

the darkened
pane

exactly
down the center

is
transfixed

THIS IS JUST TO SAY

I have eaten
the plums
that were in
the icebox

and which
you were probably
saving
for breakfast

Forgive me
they were delicious
so sweet
and so cold

THE SEA-ELEPHANT

Trundled from
the strangeness of the sea –
a kind of
heaven –

Ladies and Gentlemen!
the greatest
sea-monster ever exhibited
alive

the gigantic
sea-elephant! O wallow
of flesh where
are

there fish enough for
that
appetite stupidity
cannot lessen?

Sick
of April's smallness
the little
leaves –

73

Flesh has lief of you
enormous sea –
Speak!
Blouaugh! (feed

me) my
flesh is riven –

fish after fish into his maw
unswallowing

to let them glide down
gulching back
half spittle half
brine

the
troubled eyes – torn
from the sea.
(In

a practical voice) They
ought
to put it back where
it came from.

Gape.
Strange head –
told by old sailors –
rising

bearded
to the surface – and
the only
sense out of them

is that woman's
Yes
it's wonderful but they
ought to

put it
back into the sea where
it came from.
Blouaugh!

Swing – ride
walk
on wires – toss balls
stoop and

contort yourselves –
But I
am love. I am
from the sea –

Blouaugh!
there is no crime save
the too-heavy
body

the sea
held playfully – comes
to the surface
the water

boiling
about the head the cows
scattering
fish dripping from

the bounty
of . . . and spring
they say
Spring is icummen in –

75

DEATH

He's dead
the dog won't have to
sleep on his potatoes
any more to keep them
from freezing

he's dead
the old bastard –
He's a bastard because

there's nothing
legitimate in him any
more
      he's dead
He's sick-dead

                 he's
a godforsaken curio
without
any breath in it

He's nothing at all
      he's dead
shrunken up to skin

      Put his head on
one chair and his
feet on another and
he'll lie there
like an acrobat –

Love's beaten. He
beat it. That's why
he's insufferable –

because
he's here needing a
shave and making love
an inside howl
of anguish and defeat –

He's come out of the man
and he's let
the man go –
                    the liar

Dead
         his eyes
rolled up out of
the light – a mockery

                              which
love cannot touch –

just bury it
and hide its face
for shame.

THE BOTTICELLIAN TREES

The alphabet of
the trees

is fading in the
song of the leaves

the crossing
bars of the thin

letters that spelled
winter

77

and the cold
have been illumined

with
pointed green

by the rain and sun –
The strict simple

principles of
straight branches

are being modified
by pinched-out

ifs of color, devout
conditions

the smiles of love –
. . . . . .

until the stript
sentences

move as a woman's
limbs under cloth

and praise from secrecy
quick with desire

love's ascendancy
in summer –

In summer the song
sings itself

above the muffled words –

From THE DESCENT OF WINTER

9/30

There are no perfect waves –
Your writings are a sea
full of misspellings and
faulty sentences. Level. Troubled

A center distant from the land
touched by the wings
of nearly silent birds
that never seem to rest –

This is the sadness of the sea –
waves like words, all broken –
a sameness of lifting and falling mood.

I lean watching the detail
of brittle crest, the delicate
imperfect foam, yellow weed
one piece like another –

There is no hope – if not a coral
island slowly forming
to wait for birds to drop
the seeds will make it habitable

10/21

In the dead weeds a rubbish heap
aflame: the orange flames
stream horizontal, windblown
they parallel the ground
waving up and down

the flamepoints alternating
the body streaked with loops
and purple stains while
the pale smoke, above
steadily continues eastward –

10/22

that brilliant field
of rainwet orange
blanketed

by the red grass
and oilgreen bayberry

the last yarrow
on the gutter
white by the sandy
rainwater

and a white birch
with yellow leaves
and few
and loosely hung

and a young dog
jumped out
of the old barrel

10/28

in this strong light
the leafless beechtree
shines like a cloud

it seems to glow
of itself
with a soft stript light
of love
over the brittle
grass

But there are
on second look
a few yellow leaves
still shaking

far apart

just one here one there
trembling vividly

11/1

The moon, the dried weeds
and the Pleiades –

Seven feet tall
the dark, dried weedstalks
make a part of the night
a red lace
on the blue milky sky

Write –
by a small lamp

the Pleiades are almost
nameless
and the moon is tilted
and halfgone

And in runningpants and
with ecstatic, aesthetic faces
on the illumined
signboard are leaping
over printed hurdles and
'$\frac{1}{4}$ of their energy comes from bread'

two
gigantic highschool boys
ten feet tall

AN EARLY MARTYR
[1935]

AN EARLY MARTYR

Rather than permit him
to testify in court
Giving reasons
why he stole from
Exclusive stores
then sent post-cards
To the police
to come and arrest him
– if they could –
They railroaded him
to an asylum for
The criminally insane
without trial

The prophylactic to
madness
Having been denied him
he went close to
The edge out of
frustration and
Doggedness –

Inflexible, finally they
had to release him –
The institution was
'overcrowded'
They let him go
in the custody of
A relative on condition
that he remain
Out of the state –

They 'cured' him all
right
But the set-up
he fought against
Remains –
and his youthful deed
Signalizing
the romantic period
Of a revolt·
he served well
Is still good –

Let him be
a factory whistle
That keeps blaring –
Sense, sense, sense!
so long as there's
A mind to remember
and a voice to
carry it on –

Never give up
keep at it!
Unavoided, terrifying
to such bought
Courts as he thought
to trust to but they
Double-crossed him.

FLOWERS BY THE SEA

When over the flowery, sharp pasture's
edge, unseen, the salt ocean

lifts its form – chicory and daisies
tied, released, seem hardly flowers alone

but color and the movement – or the shape
perhaps – of restlessness, whereas

the sea is circled and sways
peacefully upon its plantlike stem

ITEM

This, with a face
like a mashed blood orange
that suddenly

would get eyes
and look up and scream
War! War!

clutching her
thick, ragged coat
A piece of hat

broken shoes
War! War!
stumbling for dread

at the young men
who with their gun-butts
shove her

sprawling –
a note
at the foot of the page

THE LOCUST TREE IN FLOWER

Among
the leaves
bright

green
of wrist-thick
tree

and old
stiff broken
branch

ferncool
swaying
loosely strung –

come May
again
white blossom

clusters
hide
to spill

their sweets
almost
unnoticed

down
and quickly
fall

THE LOCUST TREE IN FLOWER

Among
of
green

stiff
old
bright

broken
branch
come

white
sweet
May

again

VIEW OF A LAKE

from a
highway below a face
of rock

too recently blasted
to be overgrown
with grass or fern:

Where a
waste of cinders
slopes down to

AN EARLY MARTYR

the railroad and
the lake
stand three children

beside the weed-grown
chassis
of a wrecked car

immobile in a line
facing the water
To the left a boy

in falling off
blue overalls
Next to him a girl

in a grimy frock
And another boy
They are intent

watching something
below – ?
A section sign: 50

on an iron post
planted
by a narrow concrete

service hut
(to which runs
a sheaf of wires)

in the universal
cinders beaten
into crossing paths

AN EARLY MARTYR

to form the front yard
of a frame house
at the right

that looks
to have been flayed
Opposite

remains a sycamore
in leaf
Intently fixed

the three
with straight backs
ignore

the stalled traffic
all eyes
toward the water

TO A POOR OLD WOMAN

munching a plum on
the street a paper bag
of them in her hand

They taste good to her
They taste good
to her. They taste
good to her

You can see it by
the way she gives herself
to the one half
sucked out in her hand

Lack of punctuation

Suggests simple mindedness

AN EARLY MARTYR

Comforted
a solace of ripe plums
seeming to fill the air
They taste good to her

PROLETARIAN PORTRAIT

A big young bareheaded woman
in an apron

Her hair slicked back standing
on the street

One stockinged foot toeing
the sidewalk

Her shoe in her hand. Looking
intently into it

She pulls out the paper insole
to find the nail

That has been hurting her

THE RAPER FROM PASSENACK

was very kind. When she regained
her wits, he said, It's all right, kid,
I took care of you.

What a mess she was in. Then he added,
You'll never forget me now.
And drove her home.

Only a man who is sick, she said
would do a thing like that.
It must be so.

No one who is not diseased could be
so insanely cruel. He wants to give it
to someone else –

to justify himself. But if I get a
venereal infection out of this
I won't be treated.

I refuse. You'll find me dead in bed
first. Why not? That's
the way she spoke,

I wish I could shoot him. How would
you like to know a murderer?
I may do it.

I'll know by the end of this week.
I wouldn't scream. I bit him
several times

but he was too strong for me.
I can't yet understand it. I don't
faint so easily.

When I came to myself and realized
what had happened all I could do
was to curse

and call him every vile name I could
think of. I was so glad
to be taken home.

I suppose it's my mind – the fear of
infection. I'd rather a million times
have been got pregnant.

But it's the foulness of it can't
be cured. And hatred, hatred of all men
– and disgust.

THE YACHTS

contend in a sea which the land partly encloses
shielding them from the too-heavy blows
of an ungoverned ocean which when it chooses

tortures the biggest hulls, the best man knows
to pit against its beatings, and sinks them pitilessly.
Mothlike in mists, scintillant in the minute

brilliance of cloudless days, with broad bellying sails
they glide to the wind tossing green water
from their sharp prows while over them the crew crawls

ant-like, solicitously grooming them, releasing,
making fast as they turn, lean far over and having
caught the wind again, side by side, head for the mark.

In a well guarded arena of open water surrounded by
lesser and greater craft which, sycophant, lumbering
and flittering follow them, they appear youthful, rare

as the light of a happy eye, live with the grace
of all that in the mind is fleckless, free and
naturally to be desired. Now the sea which holds them

is moody, lapping their glossy sides, as if feeling
for some slightest flaw but fails completely.
Today no race. Then the wind comes again. The yachts

move, jockeying for a start, the signal is set and they
are off. Now the waves strike at them but they are too
well made, they slip through, though they take in canvas.

Arms with hands grasping seek to clutch at the prows.
Bodies thrown recklessly in the way are cut aside.
It is a sea of faces about them in agony, in despair

until the horror of the race dawns staggering the mind,
the whole sea become an entanglement of watery bodies
lost to the world bearing what they cannot hold. Broken,

beaten, desolate, reaching from the dead to be taken up
they cry out, failing, failing! their cries rising
in waves still as the skillful yachts pass over.

THE CATHOLIC BELLS

Tho' I'm no Catholic
I listen hard when the bells
in the yellow-brick tower
of their new church

ring down the leaves
ring in the frost upon them
and the death of the flowers
ring out the grackle

toward the south, the sky
darkened by them, ring in
the new baby of Mr and Mrs
Krantz which cannot

for the fat of its cheeks
open well its eyes, ring out
the parrot under its hood
jealous of the child

ring in Sunday morning
and old age which adds as it
takes away. Let them ring
only ring! over the oil

painting of a young priest
on the church wall advertising
last week's Novena to St
Anthony, ring for the lame

young man in black with
gaunt cheeks and wearing a
Derby hat, who is hurrying
to 11 o'clock Mass (the

grapes still hanging to
the vine along the nearby
Concordia Halle like broken
teeth in the head of an

old man) Let them ring
for the eyes and ring for
the hands and ring for
the children of my friend

who no longer hears
them ring but with a smile
and in a low voice speaks
of the decisions of her

daughter and the proposals
and betrayals of her
husband's friends. O bells
ring for the ringing!

the beginning and the end
of the ringing! Ring ring
ring ring ring ring ring!
Catholic bells – !

ADAM AND EVE AND THE CITY
[1936]

FINE WORK WITH PITCH AND COPPER

Now they are resting
in the fleckless light
separately in unison

like the sacks
of sifted stone stacked
regularly by twos

about the flat roof
ready after lunch
to be opened and strewn

The copper in eight
foot strips has been
beaten lengthwise

down the center at right
angles and lies ready
to edge the coping

One still chewing
picks up a copper strip
and runs his eye along it

ADAM

He grew up by the sea
on a hot island
inhabited by negroes – mostly.
There he built himself
a boat and a separate room
close to the water

for a piano on which he practiced –
by sheer doggedness
and strength of purpose
striving
like an Englishman
to emulate his Spanish friend
and idol – the weather!

And there he learned
to play the flute – not very well –

Thence he was driven
out of Paradise – to taste
the death that duty brings
so daintily, so mincingly,
with such a noble air –
that enslaved him all his life
thereafter –

And he left behind
all the curious memories that come
with shells and hurricanes –
the smells
and sounds and glancing looks
that Latins know belong
to boredom and long torrid hours
and Englishmen

will never understand – whom
duty has marked
for special mention – with
a tropic of its own
and its own heavy-winged fowl
and flowers that vomit beauty
at midnight –

But the Latin has turned romance
to a purpose cold as ice.
He never sees
or seldom
what melted Adam's knees
to jelly and despair – and
held them up pontifically –

Underneath the whisperings
of tropic nights
there is a darker whispering
that death invents especially
for northern men
whom the tropics
have come to hold.

It would have been enough
to know that never,
never, never, never would
peace come as the sun comes
in the hot islands.
But there was
a special hell besides
where black women lie waiting
for a boy –

Naked on a raft
he could see the barracudas
waiting to castrate him
so the saying went –
Circumstances take longer –

But being an Englishman
though he had not lived in England
desde que avia cinco años
he never turned back
but kept a cold eye always

on the inevitable end
never wincing – never to unbend –
God's handyman
going quietly into hell's mouth
for a paper of reference –
fetching water to posterity
a British passport
always in his pocket –
muleback over Costa Rica
eating pâtés of black ants
And the Latin ladies admired him
and under their smiles
dartled the dagger of despair
in spite of
a most thorough trial –
found his English heart safe
in the roseate steel. Duty
the angel
which with whip in hand ...
– along the low wall of paradise
where they sat and smiled
and flipped their fans
at him –

He never had but the one home
Staring Him in the eye
coldly
and with patience –
without a murmur, silently
a desperate, unvarying silence
to the unhurried last.

THE CRIMSON CYCLAMEN

(To the Memory of Charles Demuth)

White suffused with red
more rose than crimson
– all acolor
the petals flare back
from the stooping craters
of those flowers
as from a wind rising –
And though the light
that enfolds and pierces
them discovers blues
and yellows there also –
and crimson's a dull word
beside such play –
yet the effect against
this winter where
they stand – is crimson –

It is miraculous
that flower should rise
by flower
alike in loveliness –
as thought mirrors
of some perfection
could never be
too often shown –
silence holds them –
in that space. And
color has been construed
from emptiness
to waken there –

But the form came gradually.
The plant was there
before the flowers
as always – the leaves,
day by day changing. In
September when the first
pink pointed bud still
bowed below, all the leaves
heart-shaped
were already spread –
quirked and green
and stenciled with a paler
green
irregularly
across and round the edge –

Upon each leaf it is
a pattern more
of logic than a purpose
links each part to the rest,
an abstraction
playfully following
centripetal
devices, as of pure thought –
the edge tying by
convergent, crazy rays
with the center –
where that dips
cupping down to the
upright stem – the source
that has splayed out
fanwise and returns
upon itself in the design
thus decoratively –

Such are the leaves
freakish, of the air

as thought is, of roots
dark, complex from
subterranean revolutions
and rank odors
waiting for the moon –
The young leaves
coming among the rest
are more crisp
and deeply cupped
the edges rising first
impatient of the slower
stem – the older
level, the oldest
with the edge already
fallen a little backward –
the stem alone
holding the form
stiffly a while longer –

Under the leaf, the same
though the smooth green
is gone. Now the ribbed
design – if not
the purpose, is explained.
The stem's pink flanges,
strongly marked,
stand to the frail edge,
dividing, thinning
through the pink and downy
mesh – as the round stem
is pink also – cranking
to penciled lines
angularly deft
through all, to link together
the unnicked argument
to the last crinkled edge –
where the under and the over

meet and disappear
and the air alone begins
to go from them –
the conclusion left still
blunt, floating
if warped and quaintly flecked
whitened and streaked
resting
upon the tie of the stem –

But half hidden under them
such as they are
it begins that must
put thought to rest –

wakes in tinted beaks
still raising the head
and passion
is loosed –

its small lusts
addressed still to
the knees and to sleep –
abandoning argument

lifts
through the leaves
day by day
and one day opens!

The petals!
the petals undone
loosen all five and
swing up

The flower
flows to release –

Fast within a ring
where the compact
agencies
of conception

lie mathematically
ranged
round the
hair-like sting –

From such a pit
the color flows
over
a purple rim

upward to
the light! the light!
all around –
Five petals

as one
to flare, inverted
a full flower
each petal tortured

eccentrically
the while, warped edge
jostling
half-turned edge

side by side
until compact, tense
evenly stained
to the last fine edge

an ecstasy
from the empurpled ring
climbs up (though
firm there still)

each petal
by excess of tensions
in its own flesh
all rose –

rose red
standing until it
bends backward
upon the rest, above,

answering
ecstasy with excess
all together
acrobatically

not as if bound
(though still bound)
but upright
as if they hung

from above
to the streams
with which
they are veined and glow –
the frail fruit
by its frailty supreme
opening in the tense moment
to no bean
no completion
no root
no leaf and no stem
but color only and a form –

It is passion
earlier and later than thought
that rises above thought
at instant peril – peril
itself a flower
that lifts and draws it on –

Frailer than level thought
more convolute
rose red
highest
the soonest to wither
blacken
and fall upon itself
formless –

And the flowers
grow older and begin
to change, larger now
less tense, when at the full
relaxing, widening
the petals falling down
the color paling
through violaceous to
tinted white –

The structure of the petal
that was all red
beginning now to show
from a deep central vein
other finely scratched veins
dwindling to that edge
through which the light
more and more shows
fading through gradations
immeasurable to the eye –

The day rises and swifter
briefer
more frailly relaxed
than thought that still
holds good – the color
draws back while still
the flower grows
the rose of it nearly all lost
a darkness of dawning purple
paints a deeper afternoon –

The day passes
in a horizon of colors
all meeting
less severe in loveliness
the petals fallen now well back
till flower touches flower
all round
at the petal tips
merging into one flower –

THE COMPLETE COLLECTED POEMS
1906–1938

[1938]

CLASSIC SCENE

A power-house
in the shape of
a red brick chair
90 feet high

on the seat of which
sit the figures
of two metal
stacks – aluminum –

commanding an area
of squalid shacks
side by side –
from one of which

buff smoke
streams while under
a grey sky
the other remains

passive today –

AUTUMN

A stand of people
by an open

grave underneath
the heavy leaves

celebrates
the cut and fill

for the new road
where

an old man
on his knees

reaps a basket-
ful of

matted grasses for
his goats

THE TERM

A rumpled sheet
of brown paper
about the length

and apparent bulk
of a man was
rolling with the

wind slowly over
and over in
the street as

a car drove down
upon it and
crushed it to

the ground. Unlike
a man it rose
again rolling

with the wind over
and over to be as
it was before.

THE SUN

lifts heavily
and cloud and sea
weigh upon the
unwaiting air –

Hasteless
the silence is
divided
by small waves

that wash away
night whose wave
is without
sound and gone –

Old categories
slacken
memoryless –
weed and shells where

in the night
a high tide left
its mark
and block of half

burned wood washed
clean –
The slovenly bearded
rocks hiss –

Obscene refuse
charms
this modern shore –
Listen!

it is a sea-snail
singing –
Relax, relent –
the sun has climbed

the sand is
drying – Lie
by the broken boat –
the eel-grass,

bends
and is released
again – Go down, go
down past knowledge

shelly lace –
among the rot
of children
screaming

their delight –
logged
in the penetrable
nothingness

whose heavy body
opens
to their leaps
without a wound –

A BASTARD PEACE

– where a heavy
woven-wire fence
topped with jagged ends, encloses
a long cinder-field by the river –

A concrete disposal tank at
one end, small wooden
pit-covers scattered about – above
sewer intakes, most probably –

Down the center's a service path
graced on one side by
a dandelion in bloom – and a white
butterfly –

The sun parches still
the parched grass. Along
the fence, blocked from the water
leans the washed-out street –

Three cracked houses –
a willow, two chickens, a
small boy, with a home-made push cart,
walking by, waving a whip –

Gid ap! No other traffic or
like to be.
There to rest, to improvise and
unbend! Through the fence

beyond the field and shining
water, 12 o'clock blows
but nobody goes
other than the kids from school –

THE POOR

It's the anarchy of poverty
delights me, the old
yellow wooden house indented
among the new brick tenements

Or a cast-iron balcony
with panels showing oak branches
in full leaf. It fits
the dress of the children

reflecting every stage and
custom of necessity –
Chimneys, roofs, fences of
wood and metal in an unfenced

age and enclosing next to
nothing at all: the old man
in a sweater and soft black
hat who sweeps the sidewalk –

his own ten feet of it
in a wind that fitfully
turning his corner has
overwhelmed the entire city

THE DEFECTIVE RECORD

Cut the bank for the fill.
Dump sand
pumped out of the river
into the old swale

killing whatever was
there before – including
even the muskrats. Who did it?
There's the guy.

Him in the blue shirt and
turquoise skullcap.
Level it down
for him to build a house

on to build a
house on to build a house on
to build a house
on to build a house on to . . .

THESE

are the desolate, dark weeks
when nature in its barrenness
equals the stupidity of man.

The year plunges into night
and the heart plunges
lower than night

to an empty, windswept place
without sun, stars or moon
but a peculiar light as of thought

that spins a dark fire –
whirling upon itself until,
in the cold, it kindles

to make a man aware of nothing
that he knows, not loneliness
itself – Not a ghost but

would be embraced – emptiness,
despair – (They
whine and whistle) among

the flashes and booms of war;
houses of whose rooms
the cold is greater than can be thought,

the people gone that we loved,
the beds lying empty, the couches
damp, the chairs unused –

Hide it away somewhere
out of the mind, let it get roots
and grow, unrelated to jealous

ears and eyes – for itself.
In this mine they come to dig – all.
Is this the counterfoil to sweetest

music? The source of poetry that
seeing the clock stopped, says,
The clock has stopped

that ticked yesterday so well?
and hears the sound of lakewater
splashing – that is now stone.

MORNING

on the hill is cool! Even the dead
grass stems that start with the wind along
the crude board fence are less than harsh.

– a broken fringe of wooden and brick fronts
above the city, fading out,
beyond the watertank on stilts,
an isolated house or two here and there,
into the bare fields.

           The sky is immensely
wide! No one about. The houses badly
numbered.

            Sun benches at the curb bespeak
another season, truncated poplars
that having served for shade
served also later for the fire. Rough
cobbles and abandoned car rails interrupted
by precipitous cross streets.

                              Down-hill
in the small, separate gardens (Keep out
you) bare fruit trees and among tangled
cords of unpruned grapevines low houses
showered by unobstructed light.

                                    Pulley lines
to poles, on one a blue
and white tablecloth bellying easily.
Feather beds from windows and swathed in
old linoleum and burlap, fig trees. Barrels
over shrubs.

                                    Level of
the hill, two old men walking and talking
come on together.

                              – Firewood, all lengths
and qualities stacked behind patched
out-houses. Uses for ashes.
And a church spire sketched on the sky,
of sheet-metal and open beams, to resemble
a church spire –

                              – These Wops are wise

                                    – and walk about

absorbed among stray dogs and sparrows,
pigeons wheeling overhead, their
feces falling –

or shawled and jug in hand
beside a concrete wall down which,
from a loose water-pipe, a stain descends,
the wall descending also, holding up
a garden – On its side the pattern of
the boards that made the forms is still
discernible. – to the oil-streaked
highway –

Whence, turn and look where,
at the crest, the shoulders of a man
are disappearing gradually below the worn
fox-fur of tattered grasses –

And round again, the
two old men in caps crossing at
a gutter now, *Pago, Pago!* still absorbed.

– a young man's face staring
from a dirty window – Women's Hats – and
at the door a cat, with one fore-foot on
the top step, looks back –

Scatubitch!

Sacks of flour
piled inside the bakery window, their
paley trade-marks flattened to
the glass –

And with a stick,
scratching within the littered field –
old plaster, bits of brick – to find what
coming? In God's name! Washed out, worn
out, scavengered and rescavengered –

Spirit of place rise from these ashes
repeating secretly an obscure refrain:

This is my house and here I live.
Here I was born and this is my office –

– passionately leans examining, stirring
with the stick, a child following.
Roots, salads? Medicinal, stomachic?
Of what sort? Abortifacient? To be dug,
split, submitted to the sun, brewed
cooled in a teacup and applied?

                              Kid Hot
Jock, in red paint, smeared along
the fence. – and still remains, of –
if and if, as the sun rises, rolls and
comes again.

                    But every day, every day
she goes and kneels –

                         died of tuberculosis
when he came back from the war, nobody
else in our family ever had it except a
baby once after that –

                              alone on the cold
floor beside the candled altar, stifled
weeping – and moans for his lost
departed soul the tears falling
and wiped away, turbid with her grime.

Covered, swaddled, pinched and saved
shrivelled, broken – to be rewhetted and
used again.

THE BROKEN SPAN
[1941]

THE LAST WORDS OF MY ENGLISH
GRANDMOTHER

1920

There were some dirty plates
and a glass of milk
beside her on a small table
near the rank, disheveled bed –

Wrinkled and nearly blind
she lay and snored
rousing with anger in her tones
to cry for food,

Gimme something to eat –
They're starving me –
I'm all right I won't go
to the hospital. No, no, no

Give me something to eat
Let me take you
to the hospital, I said
and after you are well

you can do as you please.
She smiled, Yes
you do what you please first
then I can do what I please –

Oh, oh, oh! she cried
as the ambulance men lifted
her to the stretcher –
Is this what you call

making me comfortable?
By now her mind was clear –
Oh you think you're smart
you young people,

she said, but I'll tell you
you don't know anything.
Then we started.
On the way

we passed a long row
of elms. She looked at them
awhile out of
the ambulance window and said,

What are all those
fuzzy-looking things out there?
Trees? Well, I'm tired
of them and rolled her head away.

THE PREDICTER OF FAMINE

White day, black river
corrugated and swift –

as the stone of the sky
on the prongy ring
of the tarnished city
is smooth and without motion:

A gull flies low
upstream, his beak tilted
sharply, his eye
alert to the providing water.

A PORTRAIT OF THE TIMES

Two W. P. A. men
stood in the new
sluiceway

overlooking
the river –
One was pissing

while the other
showed
by his red

jagged face the
immemorial tragedy
of lack-love

while an old
squint-eyed woman
in a black

dress
and clutching
a bunch of

late chrysanthemums
to her
fatted bosoms

turned her back
on them
at the corner

AGAINST THE SKY

Let me not forget at least,
after the three day rain,
beaks raised aface, the two starlings
at and near the top twig

of the white-oak, dwarfing
the barn, completing the minute
green of the sculptured foliage, their
bullet heads bent back, their horny

lips chattering to the morning
sun! Praise! while the
wraithlike warblers, all but unseen
in looping flight dart from

pine to spruce, spruce to pine
southward. Southward! where
new mating warms the wit and cold
does not strike, for respite.

THE WEDGE
[1944]

A SORT OF A SONG

Let the snake wait under
his weed
and the writing
be of words, slow and quick, sharp
to strike, quiet to wait,
sleepless.

– through metaphor to reconcile
the people and the stones.
Compose. (No ideas
but in things) Invent!
Saxifrage is my flower that splits
the rocks.

PATERSON: THE FALLS

What common language to unravel?
The Falls, combed into straight lines
from that rafter of a rock's
lip. Strike in! the middle of

some trenchant phrase, some
well packed clause. Then ...
This is my plan. 4 sections: First,
the archaic persons of the drama.

An eternity of bird and bush,
resolved. An unraveling:
the confused streams aligned, side
by side, speaking! Sound

married to strength, a strength
of falling – from a height! The wild
voice of the shirt-sleeved
Evangelist rivaling, Hear

me! I am the Resurrection
and the Life! echoing
among the bass and pickerel, slim
eels from Barbados, Sargasso

Sea, working up the coast to that
bounty, ponds and wild streams –
Third, the old town: Alexander Hamilton
working up from St Croix,

from that sea! and a deeper, whence
he came! stopped cold
by that unmoving roar, fastened
there: the rocks silent

but the water, married to the stone,
voluble, though frozen; the water
even when and though frozen
still whispers and moans –

And in the brittle air
a factory bell clangs, at dawn, and
snow whines under their feet. Fourth,
the modern town, a

disembodied roar! the cataract and
its clamor broken apart – and from
all learning, the empty
ear struck from within, roaring . . .

THE DANCE

In Breughel's great picture, The Kermess,
the dancers go round, they go round and
around, the squeal and the blare and the
tweedle of bagpipes, a bugle and fiddles
tipping their bellies (round as the thick-
sided glasses whose wash they impound)
their hips and their bellies off balance
to turn them. Kicking and rolling about
the Fair Grounds, swinging their butts, those
shanks must be sound to bear up under such
rollicking measures, prance as they dance
in Breughel's great picture, The Kermess.

BURNING THE CHRISTMAS GREENS

Their time past, pulled down
cracked and flung to the fire
– go up in a roar

All recognition lost, burnt clean
clean in the flame, the green
dispersed, a living red,
flame red, red as blood wakes
on the ash –

and ebbs to a steady burning
the rekindled bed become
a landscape of flame

At the winter's midnight
we went to the trees, the coarse
holly, the balsam and
the hemlock for their green

At the thick of the dark
the moment of the cold's
deepest plunge we brought branches
cut from the green trees

to fill our need, and over
doorways, about paper Christmas
bells covered with tinfoil
and fastened by red ribbons

we stuck the green prongs
in the windows hung
woven wreaths and above pictures
the living green. On the

mantle we built a green forest
and among those hemlock
sprays put a herd of small
white deer as if they

were walking there. All this!
and it seemed gentle and good
to us. Their time past,
relief! The room bare. We

stuffed the dead grate
with them upon the half burnt out
log's smoldering eye, opening
red and closing under them

and we stood there looking down.
Green is a solace
a promise of peace, a fort
against the cold (though we

did not say so) a challenge
above the snow's
hard shell. Green (we might
have said) that, where

small birds hide and dodge
and lift their plaintive
rallying cries, blocks for them
and knocks down

the unseeing bullets of
the storm. Green spruce boughs
pulled down by a weight of
snow – Transformed!

Violence leaped and appeared.
Recreant! roared to life
as the flame rose through and
our eyes recoiled from it.

In the jagged flames green
to red, instant and alive. Green!
those sure abutments . . . Gone!
lost to mind

and quick in the contracting
tunnel of the grate
appeared a world! Black
mountains, black and red – as

yet uncolored – and ash white,
an infant landscape of shimmering
ash and flame and we, in
that instant, lost,

breathless to be witnesses,
as if we stood
ourselves refreshed among
the shining fauna of that fire.

THE POEM

It's all in
the sound. A song.
Seldom a song. It should

be a song – made of
particulars, wasps,
a gentian – something
immediate, open

scissors, a lady's
eyes – waking
centrifugal, centripetal

THE SEMBLABLES

The red brick monastery in
the suburbs over against the dust–
hung acreage of the unfinished
and all but subterranean

munitions plant: those high
brick walls behind which at Easter
the little orphans and bastards
in white gowns sing their Latin

responses to the hoary ritual
while frankincense and myrrh
round out the dark chapel making
an enclosed sphere of it

of which they are the worm:
that cell outside the city beside
the polluted stream and dump
heap, uncomplaining, and the field

of upended stones with a photo
under glass fastened here and there
to one of them near the deeply
carved name to distinguish it:

that trinity of slate gables
the unembellished windows piling
up, the chapel with its round
window between the dormitories

peaked by the bronze belfry
peaked in turn by the cross,
verdegris – faces all silent
that miracle that has burst sexless

from between the carrot rows.
Leafless white birches, their
empty tendrils swaying in
the all but no breeze guard

behind the spiked monastery fence
the sacred statuary. But ranks
of brilliant car-tops row on row
give back in all his glory the

late November sun and hushed
attend, before that tumbled
ground, those sightless walls
and shovelled entrances where no

one but a lonesome cop swinging
his club gives sign, that agony
within where the wrapt machines
are praying . . .

THE STORM

A perfect rainbow! a wide
arc low in the northern sky
spans the black lake

troubled by little waves
over which the sun
south of the city shines in

coldly from the bare hill
supine to the wind which
cannot waken anything

but drives the smoke from
a few lean chimneys streaming
violently southward

THE FORGOTTEN CITY

When with my mother I was coming down
from the country the day of the hurricane,
trees were across the road and small branches
kept rattling on the roof of the car
There was ten feet or more of water
making the parkways impassible with wind
bringing more rain in sheets. Brown torrents
gushed up through new sluices in the
valley floor so that I had to take what road
I could find bearing to the south and west,
to get back to the city. I passed through
extraordinary places, as vivid as any
I ever saw where the storm had broken
the barrier and let through
a strange commonplace: Long, deserted avenues

with unrecognized names at the corners and
drunken looking people with completely
foreign manners. Monuments, institutions
and in one place a large body of water
startled me with an acre or more of hot
jets spouting up symmetrically over it. Parks.
I had no idea where I was and promised myself
I would some day go back to study this
curious and industrious people who lived
in these apartments, at these sharp
corners and turns of intersecting avenues
with so little apparent communication
with an outside world. How did they get
cut off this way from representation in our
newspapers and other means of publicity
when so near the metropolis, so closely
surrounded by the familiar and the famous?

THE YELLOW CHIMNEY

There is a plume
of fleshpale
smoke upon the blue

sky. The silver
rings that
strap the yellow

brick stack at
wide intervals shine
in this amber

light – not
of the sun not of
the pale sun but

his born brother
the
declining season

THE BARE TREE

The bare cherry tree
higher than the roof
last year produced
abundant fruit. But how
speak of fruit confronted
by that skeleton?
Though live it may be
there is no fruit on it.
Therefore chop it down
and use the wood
against this biting cold.

THE CLOUDS
[1948]

FRANKLIN SQUARE

Instead of
the flower of the hawthorn
the spine:

The tree is in bloom
the flowers
and the leaves together

sheltering
the noisy sparrows
that give

by their intimate
indifference,
the squirrels and pigeons

on the sharp-
edged lawns – the figure
of a park:

A city, a decadence
of bounty –
a tall negress approaching

the bench
pursing her old mouth
for what coin?

LABRADOR

How clean these shallows
how firm these rocks stand
about which wash
the waters of the world

It is ice to this body
that unclothes its pallors
to thoughts
of an immeasurable sea,

unmarred, that as it lifts
encloses this
straining mind, these
limbs in a single gesture.

A WOMAN IN FRONT OF A BANK

The bank is a matter of columns,
like. convention,
unlike invention; but the pediments
sit there in the sun

to convince the doubting of
investments 'solid
as rock' – upon which the world
stands, the world of finance,

the only world: Just there,
talking with another woman while
rocking a baby carriage
back and forth stands a woman in

a pink cotton dress, bare legged
and headed whose legs
are two columns to hold up
her face, like Lenin's (her loosely

arranged hair profusely blond) or
Darwin's and there you
have it:
a woman in front of a bank

THE BITTER WORLD OF SPRING

On a wet pavement the white sky recedes
mottled black by the inverted
pillars of the red elms,
in perspective, that lift the tangled

net of their desires hard into
the falling rain. And brown smoke
is driven down, running like
water over the roof of the bridge-

keeper's cubicle. And, as usual,
the fight as to the nature of poetry
– Shall the philosophers capture it? –
is on. And, casting an eye

down into the water, there, announced
by the silence of a white
bush in flower, close
under the bridge, the shad ascend,

midway between the surface and the mud,
and you can see their bodies
red-finned in the dark
water headed, unrelenting, upstream.

THE BANNER BEARER

In the rain, the lonesome
dog idiosyn-
cratically, with each
quadribeat, throws

out the left fore-
foot beyond
the right intent, in
his stride,

on some obscure
insistence – from bridge-
ward going
into new territory.

HIS DAUGHTER

Her jaw wagging
her left hand pointing
stiff armed
behind her, I noticed:

her youth, her
receding chin and
fair hair;
her legs, bare

The sun was on her
as she came
to the step's edge,
the fat man,

caught in his stride,
collarless,
turned sweating
toward her.

THE MANOEUVRE

I saw the two starlings
coming in toward the wires.
But at the last,
just before alighting, they

turned in the air together
and landed backwards!
that's what got me – to
face into the wind's teeth.

THE HORSE

The horse moves
independently
without reference
to his load

He has eyes
like a woman and
turns them
about, throws

back his ears
and is generally
conscious of
the world. Yet

THE CLOUDS

he pulls when
he must and
pulls well, blowing
fog from

his nostrils
like fumes from
the twin
exhausts of a car.

HARD TIMES

Stone steps, a solid
block too tough
to be pried out, from
which the house,

rather, has been
avulsed leaving
a pedestal, on which
a fat boy in

an old overcoat, a
butt between
his thick lips, the
coat pushed back,

stands kidding,
Parking Space! three
steps up from his
less lucky fellows.

THE MOTOR-BARGE

The motor-barge is
at the bridge the
air lead
the broken ice

unmoving. A gull,
the eternal
gull, flies as
always, eyes alert

beak pointing
to the life-giving
water. Time
falters but for

the broad river-
craft which
low in the water
moves grad-

ually, edging
between the smeared
bulkheads,
churning a mild

wake, laboring
to push past
the constriction
with its heavy load

THE WELL DISCIPLINED BARGEMAN

The shadow does not move. It is the water moves,
running out. A monolith of sand on a passing barge,
riding the swift water, makes that its fellow.

Standing upon the load the well disciplined bargeman
rakes it carefully, smooth on top with nicely squared
edges to conform to the barge outlines – ritually: sand.

All about him the silver water, fish-swift, races
under the Presence. Whatever there is else is moving.
The restless gulls, unlike companionable pigeons,

taking their cue from the ruffled water, dip and circle
avidly into the gale. Only the bargeman raking
upon his barge remains, like the shadow, sleeping

RAINDROPS ON A BRIAR

I, a writer, at one time hipped on
painting, did not consider
the effects, painting,
for that reason, static, on

the contrary the stillness of
the object – the flowers, the gloves –
freed them precisely by that
from a necessity merely to move

in space as if they had been –
not children! but the thinking male
or the charged and deliver-
ing female frantic with ecstasies;

served rather to present, for me,
a more pregnant motion: a
series of varying leaves
clinging still, let us say, to

the cat-briar after last night's
storm, its waterdrops
ranged upon the arching stems
irregularly as an accompaniment.

SUZANNE

Brother Paul! look!
– but he rushes to a different
window.
The moon!

I heard shrieks and thought:
What's that?

That's just Suzanne
talking to the moon!
Pounding on the window
with both fists:

    Paul!   Paul!

– and talking to the moon.
Shrieking
and pounding the glass
with both fists!

Brother Paul! the moon!

THE MIND HESITANT

Sometimes the river
becomes a river in the mind
or of the mind
or in and of the mind

Its banks snow
the tide falling a dark
rim lies between
the water and the shore

And the mind hesitant
regarding the stream
senses
a likeness which it

will find – a complex
image: something
of white brows
bound by a ribbon

of sooty thought
beyond, yes well beyond
the mobile features
of swiftly

flowing waters, before
the tide will
change
and rise again, maybe

PHILOMENA ANDRONICO

With the boys busy
at ball
in the worn lot
nearby

She stands in
the short street
reflectively bouncing
the red ball

Slowly
practiced
a little awkwardly
throwing one leg over

(Not as she had done
formerly
screaming and
missing

But slowly
surely) then
pausing throws
the ball

With a full slow
very slow
and easy motion
following through

With a slow
half turn –
as the ball flies
and rolls gently

At the child's feet
waiting –
and yet he misses
it and turns

And runs while she
slowly
regains her former
pose

Then shoves her fingers
up through
her loose short hair
quickly

Draws one stocking
tight and
waiting
tilts

Her hips and
in the warm still
air lets
her arms
                    Fall

Fall
loosely
(waiting)
at her sides

THE COLLECTED LATER POEMS

[1950]

EVERY DAY

Every day that I go out to my car
I walk through a garden
and wish often that Aristotle
had gone on
to a consideration of the dithyrambic
poem – or that his notes had survived

Coarse grass mars the fine lawn
as I look about right and left
tic toc –
And right and left the leaves
upon the yearling peach grow along
the slender stem

No rose is sure. Each is one rose
and this, unlike another,
opens flat, almost as a saucer without
a cup. But it is a rose, rose
pink. One can feel it turning slowly
upon its thorny stem

A NOTE

When the cataract dries up, my dear
all minds attend it.
There is nothing left. Neither sticks
nor stones can build it up again
nor old women with their rites of green twigs

Bending over the remains, a body
struck through the breast bone
with a sharp spear – they have borne him

159

to an ingle at the wood's edge
from which all maidenhood is shent

– though he roared
once the cataract is dried up and done.
What rites can do to keep alive
the memory of that flood they will do
then bury it, old women that they are,
secretly where all male flesh is buried.

SEAFARER

The sea will wash in
but the rocks – jagged ribs
riding the cloth of foam
or a knob or pinnacles
          with gannets –
are the stubborn man.

He invites the storm, he
lives by it! instinct
with fears that are not fears
but prickles of ecstasy,
a secret liquor, a fire
that inflames his blood to
coldness so that the rocks
seem rather to leap
at the sea than the sea
to envelop them. They strain
forward to grasp ships
or even the sky itself that
bends down to be torn
upon them. To which he says,
It is I! I who am the rocks!
Without me nothing laughs.

THE SOUND OF WAVES

A quatrain? Is that
the end I envision?
Rather the pace
which travel chooses.

Female? Rather the end
of giving and receiving
– of love: love surmounted
is the incentive.

Hardly. The incentive
is nothing surmounted,
the challenge lying
                    elsewhere.

No end but among words
looking to the past,
plaintive and unschooled,
wanting a discipline

But wanting
more than discipline
a rock to blow upon
as a mist blows

or rain is driven
against some
headland jutting into
a sea – with small boats
perhaps riding under it
while the men fish
there, words blowing in
taking the shape of stone

.   .   .   .   .

Past that, past the image:
a voice!
out of the mist
above the waves and

the sound of waves, a
voice   .   speaking!

THE HARD CORE OF BEAUTY

The most marvellous is not
                        the beauty, deep as that is,
but the classic attempt
                        at beauty,
at the swamp's center: the
                        dead-end highway, abandoned
when the new bridge went in finally.
                        There, either side an entry
from which, burned by the sun,
                        the paint is peeling –
two potted geraniums .
                        Step inside: on a wall, a
painted plaque showing
                        ripe pomegranates .
– and, leaving, note
                        down the road – on a thumbnail,
you could sketch it on a thumbnail –
                        stone steps climbing
full up the front to
                        a second floor
minuscule
                        portico
peaked like the palate
                        of a child! God give us again
such assurance.
                There are

162

rose bushes either side
this entrance and plum trees
(one dead) surrounded
at the base by worn-out auto-tire
casings! for what purpose
but the glory of the Godhead
that poked
her twin shoulders, supporting
the draggled blondness
of her tresses, from beneath
the patient waves.
And we? the whole great world abandoned
for nothing at all, intact,
the lost world of symmetry
and grace: bags of charcoal
piled deftly under
the shed at the rear, the
ditch at the very rear a passageway
through the mud,
triumphant! to pleasure,
pleasure; pleasure by boat,
a by-way of a Sunday
to the smooth river.

THE LESSON

The hydrangea
pink cheeked nods its head
a paper brain
without a skull

a brain intestined
to the invisible root
where
beside the rose and acorn

thought lies communal
with
the brooding worm
True but the air

remains
the wanton the dancing
that
holding enfolds it

a flower
aloof
Flagrant as a flag
it shakes that seamy head

or
snaps it drily
from the anchored stem
and sets it rolling

FROM TWO PENDANTS FOR THE EARS

ELENA

You lean the head forward
and wave the hand,
with a smile,
twinkling the fingers
    I say to myself
    Now it is spring
    Elena is dying

What snows, what snow
enchained her –
she of the tropics
is melted
    now she is dying

The mango, the guava
long forgot for
apple and cherry
wave good-bye
    now it is spring
    Elena is dying
        Good-bye

You think she's going to die?
said the old boy.
She's not going to die – not now.
In two days she'll be
all right again. When she dies
she'll   .

    If only she wouldn't
exhaust herself, broke in
the sturdy woman, his wife. She
fights so. You can't quieten her.

When she dies she'll go out
like a light. She's done it now
two or three times when
the wife's had her up, absolutely
out. But so far she's always
come out of it.
    Why just an hour ago
she sat up straight on that bed, as
straight as ever I saw her
in the last ten years, straight
as a ram-rod. You wouldn't believe
that would you? She's not
going to die   .   she'll be
raising Cain, looking for her grub
as per usual in the next two
or three days, you wait and see

Listen, I said, I met a man
last night told me what he'd brought
home from the market:

      2 partridges
      2 Mallard ducks
      a Dungeness crab
      24 hours out
      of the Pacific
      and 2 live-frozen
      trout
      from Denmark

What about that?

Elena is dying (I wonder)
willows and pear trees
whose encrusted branches
blossom all a mass
attend her on her way –

a guerdon
      (a garden)
       and cries of children
    indeterminate
Holy, holy, holy

            (no ritual
but fact   . in fact)

      until
the end of time (which is now)

How can you weep for her? I
cannot, I her son – though
I could weep for her without
compromising the covenant

                    She will go alone.
– or pat to the times: go wept
by a clay statuette
            (if there be miracles)
a broken head of a small
St Anne who wept at a kiss
from a child:
            She was so lonely

And Magazine # 1 sues Magazine
2, no less guilty – for libel
or infringement or dereliction
or confinement

Elena is dying (but perhaps
not yet)

Pis-en-lit attend her (I see
the children have been here)

Said Jowles, from under the
Ionian sea: What do you think
about that miracle, Doc? – that
little girl kissing
the head of that statue and making
it cry?

                            I hadn't
seen it.
                It's in the papers,
tears came out of the eyes.
I hope it doesn't turn
out to be something funny.

Let's see now: St Anne
is the grandmother of Jesus. So
that makes St Anne the mother

of the Virgin Mary

      M's a great letter, I confided.

What's that? So now it gets
to be Easter – you never know.

      Never. No, never.

The river, throwing off sparks
in a cold world

      Is this a private foight
          or kin I get into it?

This is a private fight.

      Elena is dying.
In her delirium she said
a terrible thing:

Who are you? NOW!
I, I, I, I stammered. I
am your son.

Don't go. I am unhappy.

About what? I said

About what is what.

The woman (who was watching)
added:
She thinks I'm her father.

Swallow it now: she wants
to do it herself.

      Let her spit.

At last! she said two days later
coming to herself and seeing me:

      – but I've been here
every day, Mother.

                Well why don't
they put you where I can see you
then?

    She was crying this morning,
said the woman, I'm glad you came.

           Let me clean your
glasses.

        They put them on my nose!
They're trying to make a monkey
out of me.

      Were you thinking
of La Fontaine?

        Can't you give me
something to make me disappear
completely, said she sobbing – but
completely!

       No I can't do that
Sweetheart (You God damned belittling
fool, said I to myself)

There's a little Spanish wine,
pajarete
      p-a-j-a-r-e-t-e
But pure Spanish! I don't suppose
they have it any more.

(The woman started to move her)

But I have to see my chil

Let me straighten you

I don't want the hand (my hand)
there (on her forehead)
– digging the nail of
her left thumb hard into my flesh,
the back of my own thumb
holding her hand   .   .   .

'If I had a dog ate meat
on Good Friday I'd kill him.'
said someone off to the left

Then after three days:
I'm glad to see you up and doing,
said she to me brightly.

I told you she wasn't going to
die, that was just a remission,
I think you call it, said
the 3 day beard in a soiled
undershirt

I'm afraid I'm not much use
to you, Mother, said I feebly.
I brought you a bottle of wine

– a little late for Easter

Did you? What kind of wine?
A light wine?

Sherry.

What?

Jeres. You know, *jerez.* Here
              (giving it to her)

So big! That will be my baby
now!
        (cuddling it in her arms)
Ave Maria Purissime! It is heavy!
I wonder if I could take
a little glass of it now?

                        Has
she eaten anything yet?

                        Has
she eaten anything yet!

Six oysters – she said
she wanted some fish and that's
all we had. A round
of bread and butter and a
banana
                    My God!

– two cups of tea and some
ice-cream.

        Now she wants the wine.

Will it hurt her?

                    No, I think
nothing will hurt her.

                    She's
one of the wonders of the world
I think, said his wife.

(To make the language
record it, facet to facet
not bored out –
                    with an auger.

– to give also the unshaven,
                    the rumblings of a
catastrophic past, a delicate
defeat – vivid simulations of
the mystery   .   )

We had leeks for supper, I said
What?

        Leeks! Hulda
gave them to me, they were going
to seed, the rabbits had
eaten everything else. I never
tasted better – from Pop's old
garden   .

        Pop's old what?

I'll have to clean out her ears

So my year is ended. Tomorrow
it will be April, the glory gone
the hard-edged light elapsed. Were
it not for the March within me,
the intensity of the cold sun, I
could not endure the drag
of the hours opposed to that weight,
the profusion to come later, that
comes too late. I have already
swum among the bars, the angular
contours, I have already lived
the year through

Elena is dying

The canary, I said, comes and sits
on our table in the morning
at breakfast, I mean walks about
on the table with us there
and pecks at the table-cloth

          He must
be a smart little bird

          Good-bye!

THE DESERT MUSIC
[1954]

TO DAPHNE AND VIRGINIA

The smell of the heat is boxwood
        when rousing us
                a movement of the air
stirs our thoughts
        that had no life in them
                to a life, a life in which
two women agonize:
        to live and to breathe is no less.
                Two young women.
The box odor
        is the odor of that of which
                partaking separately,
each to herself
        I partake also
                . . separately.

Be patient that I address you in a poem,
        there is no other
                fit medium.
The mind
        lives there. It is uncertain,
                can trick us and leave us
agonized. But for resources
        what can equal it?
                There is nothing. We
should be lost
        without its wings to
                fly off upon.

The mind is the cause of our distresses
        but of it we can build anew.
                Oh something more than
it flies off to:

a woman's world,
                of crossed sticks, stopping
thought. A new world
        is only a new mind.
                And the mind and the poem
are all apiece.
            Two young women
                    to be snared,
odor of box,
            to bind and hold them
                    for the mind's labors.

All women are fated similarly
            facing men
                    and there is always
another, such as I,
            who loves them,
                    loves all women, but
finds himself, touching them,
            like other men,
                    often confused.

I have two sons,
            the husbands of these women,
                    who live also
in a world of love,
        apart.
                    Shall this odor of box in
                    the heat
not also touch them
            fronting a world of women
                    from which they are
debarred
            by the very scents which draw them on
                    against easy access?
In our family we stammer unless,
        half mad,
                    we come to speech at last

And I am not
        a young man.
                My love encumbers me.
It is a love
        less than
                a young man's love but,
like this box odor
        more penetrant, infinitely
                more penetrant,
in that sense not to be resisted.

There is, in the hard
        give and take
                of a man's life with
                a woman
a thing which is not the stress itself
        but beyond
                and above
that,
        something that wants to rise
                and shake itself
free. We are not chickadees
        on a bare limb
                with a worm in the mouth.
The worm is in our brains
        and concerns them
                and not food for our
offspring, wants to disrupt
        our thought
                and throw it
to the newspapers
        or anywhere.
                There is, in short,
a counter stress,
        born of the sexual shock,
                which survives it
consonant with the moon,

to keep its own mind.
                    There is, of course,
more.
        Women
                are not alone
in that. At least
                while this healing odor is abroad
                        one can write a poem.

Staying here in the country
                on an old farm
                        we eat our breakfasts
on a balcony under an elm.
                The shrubs below us
                        are neglected. And
there, penned in
                or he would eat the garden,
                        lives a pet goose who
tilts his head
                sidewise
                        and looks up at us,
a very quiet old fellow
                who writes no poems.
                        Fine mornings we sit there
while birds
                come and go.
                        A pair of robins
is building a nest   .
                for the second time
                        this season. Men
against their reason
                speak of love, sometimes,
                        when they are old. It is
all they can do   .
                or watch a heavy goose
                        who waddles, slopping
                        noisily in the mud of
                        his pool.

THE ORCHESTRA

The precise counterpart
        of a cacophony of bird calls
                lifting the sun almighty
into his sphere: wood-winds
        clarinet and violins
                sound a prolonged A!
Ah! the sun, the sun! is about to rise
        and shed his beams
                as he has always done
upon us all,
        drudges and those
                who live at ease,
women and men,
        upon the old,
                upon children and the sick
who are about to die and are indeed
        dead in their beds,
                to whom his light
is forever lost. The cello
        raises his bass note
                manfully in the treble din:
Ah, ah and ah!
        together, unattuned
                seeking a common tone.
Love is that common tone
        shall raise his fiery head
                and sound his note.

The purpose of an orchestra
        is to organize those sounds
                and hold them
to an assembled order   .
        in spite of the
                'wrong note.' Well, shall we
think or listen? Is there a sound addressed

not wholly to the ear?
We half close
our eyes. We do not
hear it through our eyes.
It is not
a flute note either, it is the relation
of a flute note
to a drum. I am wide
awake. The mind
is listening. The ear
is alerted. But the ear
in a half-reluctant mood
stretches
.   .   and yawns.
And so the banked violins
in three tiers
enliven the scene,
pizzicato. For a short
memory or to
make the listener listen
the theme is repeated
stressing a variant:
it is a principle of music
to repeat the theme. Repeat
and repeat again,
as the pace mounts. The
theme is difficult   .
but no more difficult
than the facts to be
resolved. Repeat
and repeat the theme
and all it develops to be
until thought is dissolved
in tears.
Our dreams
have been assaulted

by a memory that will not
      sleep. The
French horns
    interpose
           .   .   their voices:
I love you. My heart
      is innocent. And this
           the first day of the world!
Say to them:
'Man has survived hitherto because he was too ignorant
to know how to realize his wishes. Now that he can realize
them, he must either change them or perish.'

Now is the time   .
           in spite of the 'wrong note'
                I love you. My heart is
innocent.
      And this the first
           (and last) day of the world

The birds twitter now anew
      but a design
           surmounts their twittering.
It is a design of a man
      that makes them twitter.
           It is a design.

THE HOST

According to their need,
      this tall Negro evangelist
           (at a table separate from the
           rest of his party);
these two young Irish nuns
      (to be described subsequently);
           and this white-haired Anglican

have come witlessly
        to partake of the host
                laid for them (and for me)
by the tired waitresses.

It is all
        (since eat we must)
                made sacred by our common need.
The evangelist's assistants
        are most open in their praise
                though covert
as would be seemly
        in such a public
                place. The nuns
are all black, a side view.
        The cleric,
                his head bowed to reveal
his unruly poll
        dines alone.

My eyes are restless.
        The evangelists eat well,
                fried oysters and what not
at this railway restaurant. The Sisters
        are soon satisfied. One
                on leaving,
looking straight before her under steadfast brows,
        reveals
                blue eyes. I myself
have brown eyes
        and a milder mouth.

There is nothing to eat,
        seek it where you will,
                but of the body of the Lord.
The blessed plants
        and the sea, yield it
                to the imagination

intact. And by that force
            it becomes real,
                        bitterly
to the poor animals
            who suffer and die
                        that we may live.

The well-fed evangels,
            the narrow-lipped and bright-eyed nuns,
                        the tall,
white-haired Anglican,
            proclaim it by their appetites
                        as do I also,
chomping with my worn-out teeth:
            the Lord is my shepherd
                        I shall not want.

No matter how well they are fed,
            how daintily
                        they put the food to their lips,
it is all
            according to the imagination!
Only the imagination
            is real! They have imagined it,
                        therefore it is so:
of the evangels,
            with the long legs characteristic of the race –
                        only the docile women
of the party smiled at me
            when, with my eyes
                        I accosted them.
The nuns – but after all
            I saw only a face, a young face
                        cut off at the brows.
It was a simple story.
            The cleric, plainly
                        from a good school,

interested me more,
      a man with whom I might
            carry on a conversation.

No one was there
      save only for
            the food. Which I alone,
being a poet,
      could have given them.
            But I
had only my eyes
      with which to speak.

JOURNEY TO LOVE
[1955]

THE IVY CROWN

The whole process is a lie,
      unless,
              crowned by excess,
it break forcefully,
      one way or another,
              from its confinement –
or find a deeper well.
      Antony and Cleopatra
           were right;
they have shown
      the way. I love you
           or I do not live
at all.

Daffodil time
      is past. This is
            summer, summer!
the heart says,
      and not even the full of it.
           No doubts
are permitted –
      though they will come
           and may
before our time
      overwhelm us.
           We are only mortal
but being mortal
      can defy our fate.
           We may
by an outside chance
      even win! We do not
           look to see
jonquils and violets

come again
　　　　but there are,
still,
　　the roses!

Romance has no part in it.
　　　The business of love is
　　　　　cruelty *which*,
by our wills,
　　　we transform
　　　　　to live together.
It has its seasons,
　　　for and against,
　　　　　whatever the heart
fumbles in the dark
　　　to assert
　　　　　toward the end of May.
Just as the nature of briars
　　　is to tear flesh,
　　　　　I have proceeded
through them.
　　　Keep
　　　　　the briars out,
they say.
　　　You cannot live
　　　　　and keep free of
briars.

Children pick flowers.
　　　Let them.
　　　　　Though having them
in hand
　　　they have no further use for them
　　　　　but leave them crumpled
at the curb's edge.

At our age the imagination
            across the sorry facts
                        lifts us
to make roses
            stand before thorns.
                        Sure
love is cruel
            and selfish
                        and totally obtuse –
at least, blinded by the light,
            young love is.
                        But we are older,
I to love
            and you to be loved,
                        we have,
no matter how,
            by our wills survived
                        to keep
the jeweled prize
            always
                        at our finger tips.
We will it so
            and so it is
                        past all accident.

THE SPARROW

(*To My Father*)

This sparrow
            who comes to sit at my window
                        is a poetic truth
more than a natural one.
            His voice,
                        his movements,

his habits –
  how he loves to
      flutter his wings
in the dust –
  all attest it;
      granted, he does it
to rid himself of lice
  but the relief he feels
      makes him
cry out lustily –
  which is a trait
      more related to music
than otherwise.
  Wherever he finds himself
      in early spring,
on back streets
  or beside palaces,
      he carries on
unaffectedly
  his amours.
      It begins in the egg,
his sex genders it:
  What is more pretentiously
      useless
or about which
  we more pride ourselves?
      It leads as often as not
to our undoing.
  The cockerel, the crow
      with their challenging voices
cannot surpass
  the insistence
      of his cheep!
Once
  at El Paso
      toward evening,
I saw – and heard! –

192

ten thousand sparrows
who had come in from
the desert
to roost. They filled the trees
of a small park. Men fled
(with ears ringing!)
from their droppings,
leaving the premises
to the alligators
who inhabit
the fountain. His image
is familiar
as that of the aristocratic
unicorn, a pity
there are not more oats eaten
nowadays
to make living easier
for him.
At that,
his small size,
keen eyes,
serviceable beak
and general truculence
assure his survival –
to say nothing
of his innumerable
brood.
Even the Japanese
know him
and have painted him
sympathetically,
with profound insight
into his minor
characteristics.
Nothing even remotely
subtle
about his lovemaking.

He crouches
before the female,
            drags his wings,
                        waltzing,
throws back his head
            and simply –
                        yells! The din
is terrific.
            The way he swipes his bill
                        across a plank
to clean it,
            is decisive.
                        So with everything
he does. His coppery
            eyebrows
                        give him the air
of being always
            a winner – and yet
                        I saw once,
the female of his species
            clinging determinedly
                        to the edge of
a water pipe,
            catch him
                        by his crown-feathers
to hold him
            silent,
                        subdued,
hanging above the city streets
            until
                        she was through with him.
What was the use
            of that?
                        She hung there
herself,
            puzzled at her success.

                          I laughed heartily.
Practical to the end,
            it is the poem
                          of his existence
that triumphed
            finally;
                          a wisp of feathers
flattened to the pavement,
            wings spread symmetrically
                          as if in flight,
the head gone,
            the black escutcheon of the breast
                          undecipherable,
an effigy of a sparrow,
            a dried wafer only,
                          left to say
and it says it
            without offense,
                          beautifully;
This was I,
            a sparrow.
                          I did my best;
farewell.

TRIBUTE TO THE PAINTERS

Satyrs dance!
            all the deformities take wing
                          centaurs
leading to the rout of the vocables
            in the writings
of Gertrude
            Stein – but
                          you cannot be
an artist
            by mere ineptitude.

195

The dream
        is in pursuit!

The neat figures of
        Paul Klee
                fill the canvas
but that
        is not the work
                of a child
The cure began, perhaps,
        with the abstractions
                of Arabic art
Dürer
        with his *Melancholy*
                was aware of it –
the shattered masonry. Leonardo
        saw it,
                the obsession,
and ridiculed it
        in *La Gioconda.*
                Bosch's
congeries of tortured souls and devils
        who prey on them
                fish
swallowing
        their own entrails
Freud
        Picasso
                Juan Gris.
The letter from a friend
        saying:
                For the last
three nights
        I have slept like a baby
                without
liquor or dope of any sort!
        We know

196

that a stasis
from a chrysalis
has stretched its wings –
like a bull
or the Minotaur
or Beethoven
in the scherzo
of his 9th Symphony
stomped
his heavy feet
I saw love
mounted naked on a horse
on a swan
the back of a fish
the bloodthirsty conger eel
and laughed
recalling the Jew
in the pit
among his fellows
when the indifferent chap
with the machine gun
was spraying the heap.
He
had not yet been hit
but smiled
comforting his companions.

Dreams possess me
and the dance
of my thoughts
involving animals
the blameless beasts
and there came to me
just now
the knowledge of
the tyranny of the image
and how

men
in their designs
            have learned
                        to shatter it
whatever it may be,
            that the trouble
                        in their minds
shall be quieted,
            put to bed
                        again.

THE PINK LOCUST

I'm persistent as the pink locust,
            once admitted
                        to the garden,
you will not easily get rid of it.
            Tear it from the ground,
                        if one hair-thin rootlet
remain
            it will come again.
                        It is
flattering to think of myself
            so. It is also
                        laughable.
A modest flower,
            resembling a pink sweet-pea,
                        you cannot help
but admire it
            until its habits
                        become known.
Are we not most of us
            like that? It would be
                        too much
if the public

pried among the minutiae
of our private affairs.
Not
that we have anything to hide
but could *they*
stand it? Of course
the world would be gratified
to find out
what fools we have made of ourselves.
The question is,
would they
be generous with us –
as we have been
with others? It is,
as I say,
a flower
incredibly resilient
under attack!
Neglect it
and it will grow into a tree.
I wish I could *so* think of myself
and of what
is to become of me.
The poet himself,
what does he think of himself
facing his world?
It will not do to say,
as he is inclined to say:
Not much. The poem
would be in *that* betrayed.
He might as well answer –
'a rose is a rose
is a rose' and let it go at that.
A rose *is* a rose
and the poem equals it
if it be well made.
The poet

cannot slight himself
without slighting
his poem –
which would be
ridiculous.
Life offers
no greater reward.
And so,
like this flower,
I persist –
for what there may be in it.
I am not,
I know,
in the galaxy of poets
a rose
but *who*, among the rest,
will deny me
my place.

FROM ASPHODEL, THAT GREENY FLOWER

BOOK II

Approaching death,
as we think, the death of love,
no distinction
any more suffices to differentiate
the particulars
of place and condition
with which we have been long
familiar.
All appears
as if seen
wavering through water.
We start awake with a cry

of recognition
      but soon the outlines
            become again vague.
If we are to understand our time,
      we must find the key to it,
            not in the eighteenth
and nineteenth centuries,
      but in earlier, wilder
            and darker epochs . .
So to know, what I have to know
      about my own death,
            if it be real,
I have to take it apart.
      What does your generation think
            of Cézanne?
I asked a young artist.
      The abstractions of Hindu painting,
            he replied,
is all at the moment which interests me.
      He liked my poem
            about the parts
of a broken bottle,
      lying green in the cinders
            of a hospital courtyard.
There was also, to his mind,
      the one on gay wallpaper
            which he had heard about
but not read.
      I was grateful to him
            for his interest.
Do you remember
      how at Interlaken
            we were waiting, four days,
to see the Jungfrau
      but rain had fallen steadily.
            Then
just before train time

on a tip from one of the waitresses
we rushed
to the Gipfel Platz
and there it was!
in the distance
covered with new-fallen snow.
When I was at Granada,
I remember,
in the overpowering heat
climbing a treeless hill
overlooking the Alhambra.
At my appearance at the summit
two small boys
who had been playing
there
made themselves scarce.
Starting to come down
by a new path
I at once found myself surrounded
by gypsy women
who came up to me,
I could speak little Spanish,
and directed me,
guided by a young girl,
on my way.
These were the pinnacles.
The deaths I suffered
began in the heads
about me, my eyes
were too keen
not to see through
the world's niggardliness.
I accepted it
as my fate.
The wealthy
I defied
or not so much they,

for they have their uses,
as they who take their cues from them.
I lived
to breathe above the stench
not knowing how I in my own person
would be overcome
finally. I was lost
failing the poem.
But if I have come from the sea
it is not to be
wholly
fascinated by the glint of waves.
The free interchange
of light over their surface
which I have compared
to a garden
should not deceive us
or prove
too difficult a figure.
The poem
if it reflects the sea
reflects only
its dance
upon that profound depth
where
it seems to triumph.
The bomb puts an end
to all that.
I am reminded
that the bomb
also
is a flower
dedicated
howbeit
to our destruction.
The mere picture
of the exploding bomb

fascinates us
      so that we cannot wait
           to prostrate ourselves
before it. We do not believe
      that love
           can so wreck our lives.
The end
      will come
           in its time.
Meanwhile
      we are sick to death
           of the bomb
and its childlike
      insistence.
           Death is no answer,
no answer –
      to a blind old man
           whose bones
have the movement
      of the sea,
           a sexless old man
for whom it is a sea
      of which his verses
           are made up.
There is no power
      so great as love
           which is a sea,
which is a garden –
      as enduring
           as the verses
of that blind old man
      destined
           to live forever.
Few men believe that
      nor in the games of children.
           They believe rather
in the bomb

and shall die by
the bomb.
Compare Darwin's voyage of the *Beagle*,
a voyage of discovery if there ever was one,
to the death
incommunicado
in the electric chair
of the Rosenbergs.
It is the mark of the times
that though we condemn
what they stood for
we admire their fortitude.
But Darwin
opened our eyes
to the gardens of the world,
as *they* closed them.
Or take that other voyage
which promised so much
but due to the world's avarice
breeding hatred
through fear,
ended so disastrously;
a voyage
with which I myself am so deeply concerned,
that of the *Pinta*,
the *Niña*
and the *Santa María*.
How the world opened its eyes!
It was a flower
upon which April
had descended from the skies!
How bitter
a disappointment!
In all,
this led mainly
to the deaths I have suffered.
For there had been kindled

205

                        more minds
than that of the discoverers
                and set dancing
                        to a measure,
a new measure!
                Soon lost.
                        The measure itself
has been lost
                and we suffer for it.
                        We come to our deaths
in silence.
                The bomb speaks.
                        All suppressions,
from the witchcraft trials at Salem
                to the latest
                        book burnings
are confessions
                that the bomb
                        has entered our lives
to destroy us.
                Every drill
                        driven into the earth
for oil enters my side
                also.
                        Waste, waste!
dominates the world.
                It is the bomb's work.
                        What else was the fire
at the Jockey Club in Buenos Aires
                (*malos aires*, we should say)
                        when with Perón's connivance
the hoodlums destroyed,
                along with the books
                        the priceless Goyas
that hung there?
                You know how we treasured
                        the few paintings

we still cling to
           especially the one
                     by the dead
Charlie Demuth.
           With your smiles
                     and other trivia of the sort
my secret life
           has been made up,
                     some baby's life
which had been lost
                     had I not intervened.
                     But the words
made solely of air
           or less,
                     that came to me
out of the air
           and insisted
                     on being written down,
I regret most –
           that there has come an end
                     to them.
For in spite of it all,
           all that I have brought on myself,
                     grew that single image
that I adore
           equally with you
                     and so
it brought us together.

PICTURES FROM BRUEGHEL

[1962]

PICTURES FROM BRUEGHEL

I SELF-PORTRAIT

In a red winter hat blue
eyes smiling
just the head and shoulders

crowded on the canvas
arms folded one
big ear the right showing

the face slightly tilted
a heavy wool coat
with broad buttons

gathered at the neck reveals
a bulbous nose
but the eyes red-rimmed

from over-use he must have
driven them hard
but the delicate wrists

show him to have been a
man unused to
manual labor unshaved his

blond beard half trimmed
no time for any-
thing but his painting

II LANDSCAPE WITH THE FALL OF ICARUS

According to Brueghel
when Icarus fell
it was spring

a farmer was ploughing
his field
the whole pageantry

of the year was
awake tingling
near

the edge of the sea
concerned
with itself

sweating in the sun
that melted
the wings' wax

unsignificantly
off the coast
there was

a splash quite unnoticed
this was
Icarus drowning

III THE HUNTERS IN THE SNOW

The over-all picture is winter
icy mountains
in the background the return

PICTURES FROM BRUEGHEL

from the hunt it is toward evening
from the left
sturdy hunters lead in

their pack the inn-sign
hanging from a
broken hinge is a stag a crucifix

between his antlers the cold
inn yard is
deserted but for a huge bonfire

that flares wind-driven tended by
women who cluster
about it to the right beyond

the hill is a pattern of skaters
Brueghel the painter
concerned with it all has chosen

a winter-struck bush for his
foreground to
complete the picture .   .

IV THE ADORATION OF THE KINGS

From the Nativity
which I have already celebrated
the Babe in its Mother's arms

the Wise Men in their stolen
splendor
and Joseph and the soldiery

attendant
with their incredulous faces
make a scene copied we'll say

from the Italian masters
but with a difference
the mastery

of the painting
and the mind the resourceful mind
that governed the whole

the alert mind dissatisfied with
what it is asked to
and cannot do

accepted the story and painted
it in the brilliant
colors of the chronicler

the downcast eyes of the Virgin
as a work of art
for profound worship

V PEASANT WEDDING

Pour the wine bridegroom
where before you the
bride is enthroned her hair

loose at her temples a head
of ripe wheat is on
the wall beside her the

guests seated at long tables
the bagpipers are ready
there is a hound under

the table the bearded Mayor
is present women in their
starched headgear are

PICTURES FROM BRUEGHEL

gabbing all but the bride
hands folded in her
lap is awkwardly silent simple

dishes are being served
clabber and what not
from a trestle made of an

unhinged barn door by two
helpers one in a red
coat a spoon in his hatband

VI HAYMAKING

The living quality of
the man's mind
stands out

and its covert assertions
for art, art, art!
painting

that the Renaissance
tried to absorb
but

it remained a wheat field
over which the
wind played

men with scythes tumbling
the wheat in
rows

the gleaners already busy
it was his own –
magpies

the patient horses no one
could take that
from him

VII THE CORN HARVEST

Summer!
the painting is organized
about a young

reaper enjoying his
noonday rest
completely

relaxed
from his morning labors
sprawled

in fact sleeping
unbuttoned
on his back

the women
have brought him his lunch
perhaps

a spot of wine
they gather gossiping
under a tree

whose shade
carelessly
he does not share the

resting
center of
their workaday world

VIII THE WEDDING DANCE IN THE OPEN AIR

Disciplined by the artist
to go round
& round

in holiday gear
a riotously gay rabble of
peasants and their

ample-bottomed doxies
fills
the market square

featured by the women in
their starched
white headgear

they prance or go openly
toward the wood's
edges

round and around in
rough shoes and
farm breeches

mouths agape
Oya!
kicking up their heels

IX THE PARABLE OF THE BLIND

This horrible but superb painting
the parable of the blind
without a red

217

in the composition shows a group
of beggars leading
each other diagonally downward

across the canvas
from one side
to stumble finally into a bog

where the picture
and the composition ends back
of which no seeing man

is represented the unshaven
features of the des—
titute with their few

pitiful possessions a basin
to wash in a peasant
cottage is seen and a church spire

the faces are raised
as toward the light
there is no detail extraneous

to the composition one
fo.lows the others stick in
hand triumphant to disaster

X CHILDREN'S GAMES

i

This is a schoolyard
crowded
with children

of all ages near a village
on a small stream
meandering by

where some boys
are swimming
bare-ass

or climbing a tree in leaf
everything
is motion

elder women are looking
after the small
fry

a play wedding a
christening
nearby one leans

hollering
into
an empty hogshead

ii

Little girls
whirling their skirts about
until they stand out flat

tops pinwheels
to run in the wind with
or a toy in 3 tiers to spin

with a piece
of twine to make it go
blindman's-buff follow the

leader stilts
high and low tipcat jacks
bowls hanging by the knees

standing on your head
run the gauntlet
a dozen on their backs

feet together kicking
through which a boy must pass
roll the hoop or a

construction
made of bricks
some mason has abandoned

iii

The desperate toys
of children
their

imagination equilibrium
and rocks
which are to be

found
everywhere
and games to drag

the other down
blindfold
to make use of

a swinging
weight
with which

at random
to bash in the
heads about

them
Brueghel saw it all
and with his grim

humor faithfully
recorded
it

SONG

beauty is a shell
from the sea
where she rules triumphant
till love has had its way with her

scallops and
lion's paws
sculptured to the
tune of retreating waves

undying accents
repeated till
the ear and the eye lie
down together in the same bed

THE WOODTHRUSH

fortunate man it is not too late
the woodthrush
flies into my garden

before the snow
he looks at me silent without
moving

his dappled breast reflecting
tragic winter
thoughts my love my own

THE POLAR BEAR

his coat resembles the snow
deep snow
the male snow
which attacks and kills

silently as it falls muffling
the world
to sleep that
the interrupted quiet return

to lie down with us
its arms
about our necks
murderously a little while

THE DANCE

When the snow falls the flakes
spin upon the long axis
that concerns them most intimately
two and two to make a dance

the mind dances with itself,
taking you by the hand,
your lover follows
there are always two,

yourself and the other,
the point of your shoe setting the pace,
if you break away and run
the dance is over

Breathlessly you will take
another partner
better or worse who will keep
at your side, at your stops

whirls and glides until he too
leaves off
on his way down as if
there were another direction

gayer, more carefree
spinning face to face but always down
with each other secure
only in each other's arms

But only the dance is sure!
make it your own.
Who can tell
what is to come of it?

in the woods of your
own nature whatever
twig interposes, and bare twigs
have an actuality of their own

this flurry of the storm
that holds us,
plays with us and discards us
dancing, dancing as may be credible.

JERSEY LYRIC

view of winter trees
before
one tree

in the foreground
where
by fresh-fallen

snow
lie 6 woodchunks ready
for the fire

TO THE GHOST OF
MARJORIE KINNAN RAWLINGS

To celebrate your brief life
as you lived it grimly
under attack as it happens
to any common soldier
black or white
surrounded by the heavy scent
of orange blossoms solitary
in your low-lying farm among the young trees

Wise and gentle-voiced
old colored women
attended you among the reeds
and polonia
with its blobs of purple
flowers your pup smelling of
skunk beside your grove-men
lovesick maids and
one friend of the same sex
who knew how to handle a boat in a swamp

Your quick trips to your
New York publisher
beating your brains out
over the composition
under the trees to the tune
of a bull got loose
gathering the fruit and
preparing new fields to be put under the plough

You lived nerves drawn
tense beside dogtooth violets
bougainvillaea swaying
rushes and yellow jasmine
that smells so sweet
young and desperate
as you were taking chances
sometimes that you should be
thrown from the saddle
and get your neck broke
as it must have happened and it did in the end

SONNET IN SEARCH OF AN AUTHOR

Nude bodies like peeled logs
sometimes give off a sweetest
odor, man and woman

under the trees in full excess
matching the cushion of

aromatic pine-drift fallen
threaded with trailing woodbine
a sonnet might be made of it

Might be made of it! odor of excess
odor of pine needles, odor of

peeled logs, odor of no odor
other than trailing woodbine that

has no odor, odor of a nude woman
sometimes, odor of a man.

PATERSON
[1946–58]

FROM BOOK ONE

'Rigor of beauty is the quest. But how will you find beauty
when it is locked in the mind past all remonstrance?'

> To make a start,
> out of particulars
> and make them general, rolling
> up the sum, by defective means –
> Sniffing the trees,
> just another dog
> among a lot of dogs. What
> else is there? And to do?
> The rest have run out –
> after the rabbits.
> Only the lame stands – on
> three legs. Scratch front and back.
> Deceive and eat. Dig
> a musty bone

> For the beginning is assuredly
> the end – since we know nothing, pure
> and simple, beyond
> our own complexities.

>   Yet there is
> no return: rolling up out of chaos,
> a nine months' wonder, the city
> the man, an identity – it can't be
> otherwise – an
> interpenetration, both ways. Rolling
> up! obverse, reverse;
> the drunk the sober; the illustrious

the gross; one. In ignorance
a certain knowledge and knowledge,
undispersed, its own undoing.

                    (The multiple seed,
packed tight with detail, soured,
is lost in the flux and the mind,
distracted, floats off in the same
scum)

Rolling up, rolling up heavy with
numbers.

                    It is the ignorant sun
rising in the slot of
hollow suns risen, so that never in this
world will a man live well in his body
save dying – and not know himself
dying; yet that is
the design. Renews himself
thereby, in addition and subtraction,
walking up and down.

                    and the craft,
subverted by thought, rolling up, let
him beware lest he turn to no more than
the writing of stale poems . . .
Minds like beds always made up,
                    (more stony than a shore)
unwilling or unable.

                    Rolling in, top up,
under, thrust and recoil, a great clatter:
lifted as air, boated, multicolored, a
wash of seas –
from mathematics to particulars –

                divided as the dew,
floating mists, to be rained down and
regathered into a river that flows
and encircles:

                shells and animalcules
generally and so to man,

                to Paterson.

THE DELINEAMENTS OF THE GIANTS

i

Paterson lies in the valley under the Passaic Falls
its spent waters forming the outline of his back. He
lies on his right side, head near the thunder
of the waters filling his dreams! Eternally asleep,
his dreams walk about the city where he persists
incognito. Butterflies settle on his stone ear.
Immortal he neither moves nor rouses and is seldom
seen, though he breathes and the subtleties of his
                machinations
drawing their substance from the noise of the pouring
                river
animate a thousand automatons. Who because they
neither know their sources nor the sills of their
disappointments walk outside their bodies aimlessly
                for the most part,
locked and forgot in their desires – unroused.

        – Say it, no ideas but in things –
nothing but the blank faces of the houses
and cylindrical trees
bent, forked by preconception and accident –
split, furrowed, creased, mottled, stained –
secret – into the body of the light!

From above, higher than the spires, higher
even than the office towers, from oozy fields
abandoned to grey beds of dead grass,
black sumac, withered weed-stalks,
mud and thickets cluttered with dead leaves –
the river comes pouring in above the city
and crashes from the edge of the gorge
in a recoil of spray and rainbow mists –

    (What common language to unravel?
     . . combed into straight lines
    from that rafter of a rock's
    lip.)

A man like a city and a woman like a flower
– who are in love. Two women. Three women.
Innumerable women, each like a flower.

                                         But
only one man – like a city.

In regard to the poems I left with you; will you be so kind as to
return them to me at my new address? And without bothering to
comment upon them if you should find that embarrassing – for it
was the human situation and not the literary one that motivated
my phone call and visit.

Besides, I know myself to be more the woman than the poet; and
to concern myself less with the publishers of poetry than with ...
living ...

But they set up an investigation ... and my doors are bolted
forever (I hope forever) against all public welfare workers, profes-
sional do-gooders and the like.

    Jostled as are the waters approaching
    the brink, his thoughts
    interlace, repel and cut under,
    rise rock-thwarted and turn aside
    but forever strain forward – or strike

an eddy and whirl, marked by a
leaf or curdy spume, seeming
to forget   .

Retake later the advance and
are replaced by succeeding hordes
pushing forward – they coalesce now
glass-smooth with their swiftness,
quiet or seem to quiet as at the close
they leap to the conclusion and
fall, fall in air! as if
floating, relieved of their weight,
split apart, ribbons; dazed, drunk
with the catastrophe of the descent
floating unsupported
to hit the rocks: to a thunder,
as if lightning had struck

All lightness lost, weight regained in
the repulse, a fury of
escape driving them to rebound
upon those coming after –
keeping nevertheless to the stream, they
retake their course, the air full
of the tumult and of spray
connotative of the equal air, coeval,
filling the void

And there, against him, stretches the low mountain.
The Park's her head, carved, above the Falls, by the quiet
river; Colored crystals the secret of those rocks;
farms and ponds, laurel and the temperate wild cactus,
yellow flowered   .   .   facing him, his
arm supporting her, by the *Valley of the Rocks*, asleep.
Pearls at her ankles, her monstrous hair
spangled with apple-blossoms is scattered about into

233

the back country, waking their dreams – where the deer run
and the wood-duck nests protecting his gallant plumage.

                    *   *   *

                    I remember
a *Geographic* picture, the 9 women
of some African chief semi-naked
astraddle a log, an official log to
be presumed, heads left:

                    Foremost
froze the young and latest,
erect, a proud queen, conscious of her power,
mud-caked, her monumental hair
slanted above the brows – violently frowning.

Behind her, packed tight up
in a descending scale of freshness
stiffened the others

                    and then   .   .
the last, the first wife,
present! supporting all the rest growing
up from her – whose careworn eyes
serious, menacing – but unabashed; breasts
sagging from hard use   .   .

Whereas the uppointed breasts
of that other, tense, charged with
pressures unrelieved   .
and the rekindling they bespoke
was evident.

                    Not that the lightnings
do not stab at the mystery of a man
from both ends – and the middle, no matter

how much a chief he may be, rather the more
because of it, to destroy him at home   .

.   .   Womanlike, a vague smile,
unattached, floating like a pigeon
after a long flight to his cote.

*   *   *

ii

There is no direction. Whither? I
cannot say. I cannot say
more than how. The how (the howl) only
is at my disposal (proposal) : watching –
colder than stone .

                    - a bud forever green,
tight-curled, upon the pavement, perfect
in juice and substance but divorced, divorced
from its fellows, fallen low –

                            Divorce is
the sign of knowledge in our time,
divorce! divorce!

                    with the roar of the river
forever in our ears (arrears)
inducing sleep and silence, the roar
of eternal sleep . . challenging
our waking –

– unfledged desire, irresponsible, green
colder to the hand than stone,
unready – challenging our waking:
Two halfgrown girls hailing hallowed Easter,
(an inversion of all out-of-doors) weaving

about themselves, from under
the heavy air, whorls of thick translucencies
poured down, cleaving them away,
shut from the light: bare-
headed, their clear hair dangling –

Two –
          disparate among the pouring
waters of their hair in which nothing is
molten –

two, bound by an instinct to be the same:
ribbons, cut from a piece,
cerise pink, binding their hair: one –
a willow twig pulled from a low
leafless bush in full bud in her hand,
(or eels or a moon!)
holds it, the gathered spray,
upright in the air, the pouring air,
strokes the soft fur –

                    Ain't they beautiful!

Certainly I am not a robin nor erudite,
no Erasmus nor bird that returns to the same
ground year by year. Or if I am   .   .
the ground has undergone
a subtle transformation, its identity altered.

Indians!
Why even speak of 'I', he dreams, which
interests me almost not at all?

                              The theme
is as it may prove: asleep, unrecognized –
all of a piece, alone
in a wind that does not move the others –

in that way: a way to spend
a Sunday afternoon while the green bush shakes.

.   .   a mass of detail
to interrelate on a new ground, difficulty;
an assonance, a homologue
                              triple piled
pulling the disparate together to clarify
and compress

The river, curling, full – as a bush shakes
and a white crane will fly
and settle later! White, in
the shallows among the blue-flowered
pickerel-weed, in summer, summer! if it should
ever come, in the shallow water!

                        On the embankment a short,
compact cone (juniper)
that trembles frantically
in the indifferent gale: male – stands
rooted there   .

The thought returns: Why have I not
but for imagined beauty where there is none
or none available, long since
put myself deliberately in the way of death?

                        Stale as a whale's breath: breath!
Breath!

        Patch leaped but Mrs Cumming shrieked
        and fell – unseen (though
        she had been standing there beside her husband half
        an hour or more twenty feet from the edge).

: a body found next spring
frozen in an ice-cake; or a body
fished next day from the muddy swirl –

both silent, uncommunicative

Only of late, late! begun to know, to
know clearly (as through clear ice) whence
I draw my breath or how to employ it
clearly – if not well:

                         Clearly!
speaks the red-breast his behest. Clearly!
clearly!

– and watch, wrapt! one branch
of the tree at the fall's edge, one
mottled branch, withheld,
among the gyrate branches
of the waist-thick sycamore,
sway less, among the rest, separate, slowly
with giraffish awkwardness, slightly
on a long axis, so slightly
as hardly to be noticed, in itself the tempest:

Thus

the first wife, with giraffish awkwardness
among thick lightnings that stab at
the mystery of a man: in sum, a sleep, a
source, a scourge   .

               on a log, her varnished hair
trussed up like a termite's nest (forming
the lines) and, her old thighs
gripping the log reverently, that,
all of a piece, holds up the others –

alert: begin to know the mottled branch
that sings   .

            certainly NOT the university,
a green bud fallen upon the pavement its
sweet breath suppressed: Divorce (the
language stutters)

                    unfledged:

two sisters from whose open mouths
Easter is born – crying aloud,

                        Divorce!

                            While

the green bush sways: is whence
I draw my breath, swaying, all of a piece,
separate, livens briefly, for the moment
unafraid   .   .

        Which is to say, though it be poorly
        said, there is a first wife
        and a first beauty, complex, ovate –
        the woody sepals standing back under
        the stress to hold it there, innate

        a flower within a flower whose history
        (within the mind) crouching
        among the ferny rocks, laughs at the names
        by which they think to trap it. Escapes!
        Never by running but by lying still –

        A history that has, by its den in the
        rocks, bole and fangs, its own cane-brake
        whence, half hid, canes and stripes
        blending, it grins (beauty defied)
        not for the sake of the encyclopedia.

                    239

Were we near enough its stinking breath
would fell us. The temple upon
the rock is its brother, whose majesty
lies in jungles – made to spring,
at the rifle-shot of learning: to kill

and grindthose bones:

These terrible things they reflect:
the snow falling into the water,
part upon the rock, part in the dry weeds
and part into the water where it
vanishes – its form no longer what it was:

the bird alighting, that pushes
its feet forward to take up the impetus
and falls forward nevertheless
among the twigs. The weak-necked daisy
bending to the wind   .   .   .

                       The sun
winding the yellow bindweed about a
bush; worms and gnats, life under a stone.
The pitiful snake with its mosaic skin
and frantic tongue. The horse, the bull
the whole din of fracturing thought
as it falls tinnily to nothing upon the streets
and the absurd dignity of a locomotive
hauling freight –

                  Pithy philosophies of
daily exits and entrances, with books
propping up one end of the shaky table –
The vague accuracies of events dancing two
and two with language which they
forever surpass – and dawns
tangled in darkness –

The giant in whose apertures we
cohabit, unaware of what air supports
us – the vague, the particular
no less vague

        his thoughts, the stream
and we, we two, isolated in the stream,
we also: three alike –

        we sit and talk
I wish to be with you abed, we two
as if the bed were the bed of a stream
– I have much to say to you

        We sit and talk,
quietly, with long lapses of silence
and I am aware of the stream
that has no language, coursing
beneath the quiet heaven of
your eyes

        which has no speech; to
go to bed with you, to pass beyond
the moment of meeting, while the
currents float still in mid-air, to
fall –
with you from the brink, before
the crash –

        to seize the moment.

We sit and talk, sensing a little
the rushing impact of the giants'
violent torrent rolling over us, a
few moments.

        If I should demand it, as
it has been demanded of others

and given too swiftly, and you should
consent. If you would consent

             We sit and talk and the
silence speaks of the giants
who have died in the past and have
returned to those scenes unsatisfied
and who is not unsatisfied, the
silent, Singac the rock-shoulder
emerging from the rocks – and the giants
live again in your silence and
unacknowledged desire –

And the air lying over the water
lifts the ripples, brother
to brother, touching as the mind touches,
counter-current, upstream
brings in the fields, hot and cold
parallel but never mingling, one that whirls
backward at the brink and curls invisibly
upward, fills the hollow, whirling,
an accompaniment – but apart, observant of
the distress, sweeps down or up clearing
the spray –

          brings in the rumors of separate
worlds, the birds as against the fish, the grape
to the green weed that streams out undulant
with the current at low tide beside the
bramble in blossom, the storm by the flood –
song and wings –

          one unlike the other, twin
of the other, conversant with eccentricities
side by side, bearing the water-drops
and snow, vergent, the water soothing the air when
it drives in among the rocks fitfully –

FROM BOOK TWO

SUNDAY IN THE PARK

i

Outside
                    outside myself
                                        there is a world,
he rumbled, subject to my incursions
- a world
                    (to me) at rest,
                                        which I approach
concretely -

        The scene's the Park
        upon the rock,
        female to the city

- upon whose body Paterson instructs his thoughts
(concretely)

                        - late spring,
        a Sunday afternoon!

- and goes by the footpath to the cliff (counting:
the proof)
                    himself among the others,
- treads there the same stones
on which their feet slip as they climb,
paced by their dogs!

laughing, calling to each other -

                    Wait for me!

.   .   the ugly legs of the young girls,
pistons too powerful for delicacy!   .
the men's arms, red, used to heat and cold,
to toss quartered beeves and   .

                    Yah! Yah! Yah! Yah!

– over-riding
                    the risks:
                                    pouring down!
For the flower of a day!

Arrived breathless, after a hard climb he,
looks back (beautiful but expensive!) to
the pearl-grey towers! Re-turns
and starts, possessive, through the trees,

                            – that love,
that is not, is not in those terms
to which I'm still the positive
in spite of all;
the ground dry, – passive-possessive

Walking –

          Thickets gather about groups of squat sand-pine,
          all but from bare rock   .   .

          – a scattering of man-high cedars (sharp cones),
          antlered sumac   .

          – roots, for the most part, writhing
          upon the surface
                              (so close are we to ruin every
          day!)
               searching the punk-dry rot

Walking –

The body is tilted slightly forward from the basic standing
position and the weight thrown on the ball of the foot,
while the other thigh is lifted and the leg and opposite
arm are swung forward (fig. 6B). Various muscles, aided

Despite my having said that I'd never write to you again, I do so
now because I find, with the passing of time, that the outcome of
my failure with you has been the complete damming up of all my
creative capacities in a particularly disastrous manner such as I have
never before experienced.

For a great many weeks now (whenever I've tried to write poetry)
every thought I've had, even every feeling, has been struck off some
surface crust of myself which began gathering when I first sensed
that you were ignoring the real contents of my last letters to you,
and which finally congealed into some impenetrable substance when
you asked me to quit corresponding with you altogether without
even an explanation.

That kind of blockage, exiling one's self from one's self – have you
ever experienced it? I dare say you have, at moments; and if so, you
can well understand what a serious psychological injury it amounts
to when turned into a permanent day-to-day condition.

How do I love you? These!

(He hears! Voices . indeterminate! Sees them
moving, in groups, by twos and fours – filtering
off by way of the many bypaths.)

 I asked him, What do you do?

 *He smiled patiently, The typical American question.
In Europe they would ask, What are you doing? Or,
What are you doing now?*

 *What do I do? I listen, to the water falling. (No
sound of it here but with the wind!) This is my entire
occupation.*

No fairer day ever dawned anywhere than May 2, 1880, when the German Singing Societies of Paterson met on Garret Mountain, as they did many years before on the first Sunday in May.

However the meeting of 1880 proved a fatal day, when William Dalzell, who owned a piece of property near the scene of the festivities, shot John Joseph Van Houten. Dalzell claimed that the visitors had in previous years walked over his garden and was determined that this year he would stop them from crossing any part of his grounds.

Immediately after the shot the quiet group of singers was turned into an infuriated mob who would take Dalzell into their own hands. The mob then proceeded to burn the barn into which Dalzell had retreated from the angry group.

Dalzell fired at the approaching mob from a window in the barn and one of the bullets struck a little girl in the cheek. . . Some of the Paterson Police rushed Dalzell out of the barn [to] the house of John Ferguson some half furlong away.

The crowd now numbered some ten thousand,

'a great beast!'

for many had come from the city to join the conflict. The case looked serious, for the Police were greatly outnumbered. The crowd then tried to burn the Ferguson house and Dalzell went to the house of John McGuckin. While in this house it was that Sergeant John McBride suggested that it might be well to send for William McNulty, Dean of Saint Joseph's Catholic Church.

In a moment the Dean set on a plan. He proceeded to the scene in a hack. Taking Dalzell by the arm, in full view of the infuriated mob, he led the man to the hack and seating himself by his side, ordered the driver to proceed. The crowd hesitated, bewildered between the bravery of the Dean and

> Signs everywhere of birds nesting, while
> in the air, slow, a crow zigzags
> with heavy wings before the wasp-thrusts
> of smaller birds circling about him
> that dive from above stabbing for his eyes

Walking –

he leaves the path, finds hard going
across-field, stubble and matted brambles
seeming a pasture – but no pasture
– old furrows, to say labor sweated or
had sweated here

                                        a flame,
spent.

            The file-sharp grass
When! from before his feet, half tripping,
picking a way, there starts
                a flight of empurpled wings!
– invisibly created (their
jackets dust-grey) from the dust kindled
to sudden ardor!

                The fly away, churring! until
their strength spent they plunge
to the coarse cover again and disappear
– but leave, livening the mind, a flashing
of wings and a churring song

AND a grasshopper of red basalt, boot-long,
tumbles from the core of his mind,
a rubble-bank disintegrating beneath a
tropic downpour

Chapultepec! grasshopper hill!

– a matt stone solicitously instructed
to bear away some rumor
of the living presence that has preceded
it, out-precedented its breath

These wings do not unfold for flight –
no need!
the weight (to the hand) finding

a counter-weight or counter buoyancy
by the mind's wings   .

He is afraid! What then?
Before his feet, at each step, the flight
is renewed. A burst of wings, a quick
churring sound   :

     couriers to the ceremonial of love!

– aflame in flight!
     – aflame only in flight!

             No flesh but the caress!

He is led forward by their announcing wings.

If that situation with you (your ignoring those particular letters and
then your final note) had belonged to the inevitable lacrimae
rerum (as did, for instance, my experience with Z.) its result could
not have been (as it *has* been) to destroy the validity for me myself
of myself, because in that case nothing to do with my sense of
personal identity would have been maimed – the cause of one's
frustrations in such instances being not *in* one's self nor in the other
person but merely in the sorry scheme of things. But since your
ignoring those letters was not 'natural' in that sense (or rather since
to regard it as unnatural I am forced, psychologically, to feel that
what I wrote you about, was sufficiently trivial and unimportant and
absurd to merit your evasion) it could not but follow that that
whole side of life connected with those letters should in consequence
take on for my own self that same kind of unreality and inaccessibility which the inner lives of other people often have for us.

      – his mind a red stone carved to be
      endless flight   .
      Love that is a stone endlessly in flight,
      so long as stone shall last bearing
      the chisel's stroke   .
      .   .   and is lost and covered
      with ash, falls from an undermined bank

and — begins churring!
AND DOES, the stone after the life!

The stone lives, the flesh dies
— we know nothing of death.

— boot long
window-eyes that front the whole head,
                    Red stone! as if
a light still clung in them   .

Love

                    combating sleep
                    _____

                    the sleep
piecemeal

Shortly after midnight, August 20, 1878, special officer Goodridge, when, in front of the Franklin House, heard a strange squealing noise down towards Ellison Street. Running to see what was the matter, he found a cat at bay under the water table at Clark's hardware store on the corner, confronting a strange black animal too small to be a cat and entirely too large for a rat. The officer ran up to the spot and the animal got in under the grating of the cellar window, from which it frequently poked its head with a lightning rapidity. Mr Goodridge made several strikes at it with his club but was unable to hit it. Then officer Keyes came along and as soon as he saw it, he said it was a mink, which confirmed the theory that Mr Goodridge had already formed. Both tried for a while to hit it with their clubs but were unable to do so, when finally officer Goodridge drew his pistol and fired a shot at the animal. The shot evidently missed its mark, but the noise and powder so frightened the little joker that it jumped out into the street, and made down into Ellison Street at a wonderful gait, closely followed by the two officers. The mink finally disappeared down a cellar window under the grocery store below Spangermacher's lager beer saloon, and that was the last seen of it. The cellar was examined again in the morning, but nothing further could be discovered of the little critter that had caused so much fun.

Without invention nothing is well spaced,
unless the mind change, unless
the stars are new measured, according
to their relative positions, the
line will not change, the necessity
will not matriculate: unless there is
a new mind there cannot be a new
line, the old will go on
repeating itself with recurring
deadliness: without invention
nothing lies under the witch-hazel
bush, the alder does not grow from among
the hummocks margining the all
but spent channel of the old swale,
the small foot-prints
of the mice under the overhanging
tufts of the bunch-grass will not
appear: without invention the line
will never again take on its ancient
divisions when the word, a supple word,
lived in it, crumbled now to chalk.

Under the bush they lie protected
from the offending sun –
11 o'clock
            They seem to talk

– a park, devoted to pleasure : devoted to   .   grasshoppers!

    3 colored girls, of age! stroll by
    – their color flagrant,
                their voices vagrant
    their laughter wild, flagillant, dissociated
    from the fixed scene   .

But the white girl, her head
upon an arm, a butt between her fingers
lies under the bush   .   .

Semi-naked, facing her, a sunshade
over his eyes,
he talks with her

– the jalopy half hid
behind them in the trees –
I bought a new bathing suit, just

pants and a brassier   :
the breasts and
the pudenda covered – beneath

the sun in frank vulgarity.
Minds beaten thin
by waste – among
the working classes SOME sort
of breakdown
has occurred. Semi-roused

they lie upon their blanket
face to face,
mottled by the shadows of the leaves

upon them, unannoyed,
at least here unchallenged.
Not undignified.   .   .

talking, flagrant beyond all talk
in perfect domesticity –
And having bathed

and having eaten (a few
sandwiches)
their pitiful thoughts do meet

in the flesh – surrounded
by churring loves! Gay wings
to bear them (in sleep)

– their thoughts alight,
away
.   .   among the grass

Walking –

across the old swale – a dry wave in the ground
tho' marked still by the line of Indian alders
.   .   they (the Indians) would weave
in and out, unseen, among them along the stream

.   come out whooping between the log
house and men working the field, cut them
off! they having left their arms in the block-
house, and – without defense – carry them away
into captivity. One old man   .

            Forget it! for God's sake, Cut
            out that stuff   .

Walking –

he rejoins the path and sees, on a treeless
knoll – the red path choking it –
a stone wall, a sort of circular
redoubt against the sky, barren and
unoccupied. Mount. Why not?

                        A chipmunk,
with tail erect, scampers among the stones.

(Thus the mind grows, up flinty pinnacles)

    but as he leans, in his stride,
  at sight of a flint arrow-head
              (it is not)
                            – there
  in the distance, to the north, appear
  to him the chronic hills   .

                    Well, so they are.
                         He stops short:
  Who's here?

            To a stone bench, to which she's leashed,
within the wall a man in tweeds – a pipe hooked in his jaw – is
combing out a new-washed Collie bitch. The deliberate comb-
strokes part the long hair – even her face he combs though her
legs tremble slightly – until it lies, as he designs, like ripples
in white sand giving off its clean-dog odor. The floor, stone
slabs, she stands patiently before his caresses in that bare 'sea
chamber'

          to the right
    from this vantage, the observation tower
    in the middle distance stands up prominently
    from its pubic grove

DEAR B. Please excuse me for not having told you this when I was
over to your house. I had no courage to answer your questions so
I'll write it. Your dog *is* going to have puppies although I prayed
she would be okey. It wasn't that she was left alone as she never
was but I used to let her out at dinner time while I hung up my
clothes. At the time, it was on a Thursday, my mother-in-law had
some sheets and table cloths out on the end of the line. I figured the
dogs wouldn't come as long as I was there and none came thru my
yard or near the apartment. He must have come between your
hedge and the house. *Every few* seconds I would run to the end of
the line or peek under the sheets to see if Musty was alright. She
was until I looked a minute too late. I took sticks and stones after
the dog but he wouldn't beat it. George gave me plenty of hell and

I started praying that I had frightened the other dog so much that
nothing had happened. I know you'll be cursing like a son-of-a-gun
and probably won't ever speak to me again for not having told
you. Don't think I haven't been worrying about Musty. She's occu-
pied my mind every day since that awful event. You won't think
so highly of me now and feel like protecting me. Instead I'll bet
you could kill . . .

        And still the picnickers come on, now
        early afternoon, and scatter through the
        trees over the fenced-in acres   .

                                Voices!
        multiple and inarticulate   .   voices
        clattering loudly to the sun, to
        the clouds. Voices!
        assaulting the air gaily from all sides.

        – among which the ear strains to catch
        the movement of one voice among the rest
        – a reed-like voice
                        of peculiar accent

        Thus she finds what peace there is, reclines,
        before his approach, stroked
        by their clambering feet – for pleasure

                        It is all for
        pleasure   .   their feet   .   aimlessly
               wandering

        The 'great beast' come to sun himself
                        as he may
        . .   their dreams mingling,
        aloof

        Let us be reasonable!
                     Sunday in the park,

limited by the escarpment, eastward; to
the west abutting on the old road: recreation
with a view! the binoculars chained
to anchored stanchions along the east wall –
     beyond which, a hawk

                    soars!

– a trumpet sounds fitfully.

Stand at the rampart (use a metronome
if your ear is deficient, one made in Hungary
if you prefer)
and look away north by east where the church
spires still spend their wits against
the sky   .   to the ball-park
in the hollow with its minute figures running
– beyond the gap where the river
plunges into the narrow gorge, unseen

– and the imagination soars, as a voice
beckons, a thundrous voice, endless
– as sleep: the voice
that has ineluctably called them –

                 that unmoving roar!
churches and factories
             (at a price)
together, summoned them from the pit   .

– his voice, one among many (unheard)
moving under all.
                 The mountain quivers.
Time! Count! Sever and mark time!

So during the early afternoon, from place
to place he moves,
his voice mingling with other voices
– the voice in his voice

opening his old throat, blowing out his lips,
kindling his mind (more
than his mind will kindle)

        – following the hikers.

At last he comes to the idlers' favorite
haunts, the picturesque summit, where
the blue-stone (rust-red where exposed)
has been faulted at various levels
        (ferns rife among the stones)
into rough terraces and partly closed in
dens of sweet grass, the ground gently sloping.

Loiterers in groups straggle
over the bare rock-table – scratched by their
boot-nails more than the glacier scratched
them – walking indifferent through
each other's privacy   .

        – in any case,
the center of movement, the core of gaiety.

Here a young man, perhaps sixteen,
is sitting with his back to the rock among
some ferns playing a guitar, dead pan   .
The rest are eating and drinking.

        The big guy
in the black hat is too full to move   .

        but Mary
is up!
      Come on! Wassa ma'? You got
broken leg?

        It is this air!

                    the air of the Midi
and the old cultures intoxicates them:
present!

        – lifts one arm holding the cymbals
of her thoughts, cocks her old head
and dances! raising her skirts:

                    La la la la!

What a bunch of bums! Afraid somebody see
you?
        Blah!
                    Escrementi!
                        – she spits.
Look a' me, Grandma! Everybody too damn
lazy.

This is the old, the very old, old upon old,
the undying: even to the minute gestures,
the hand holding the cup, the wine
spilling, the arm stained by it:

                            Remember

        the peon in the lost
        Eisenstein film drinking

        from a wine-skin with the abandon
        of a horse drinking

        so that it slopped down his chin?
        down his neck, dribbling

        over his shirt-front and down
        onto his pants – laughing, toothless?

                        Heavenly man!

– the leg raised, verisimilitude
even to the coarse contours of the leg, the
bovine touch! The leer, the cave of it,
the female of it facing the male, the satyr –
    (Priapus!)
with that lonely implication, goatherd
and goat, fertility, the attack, drunk,
cleansed   .

                Rejected. Even the film
suppressed : but   .   persistent

The picnickers laugh on the rocks celebrating
the varied Sunday of their loves with
its declining light –

Walking –

    look down (from a ledge) into this grassy
den
        (somewhat removed from the traffic)
                  above whose brows
a moon! where she lies sweating at his side:

              She stirs, distraught,
against him – wounded (drunk), moves
against him (a lump) desiring,
against him, bored   .

flagrantly bored and sleeping, a
beer bottle still grasped spear-like
in his hand   .

while the small, sleepless boys, who
have climbed the columnar rocks
overhanging the pair (where they lie
overt upon the grass, besieged –

careless in their narrow cell under
the crowd's feet) stare down,
                                    from history!
at them, puzzled and in the sexless
light (of childhood) bored equally,
go charging off   .

                              There where
the movement throbs openly
and you can hear the Evangelist shouting!
                    – moving nearer
    she – lean as a goat – leans   .
    her lean belly to the man's backside
    toying with the clips of his
    suspenders   .

– to which he adds his useless voice:
until there moves in his sleep
a music that is whole, unequivocal (in
his sleep sweating in his sleep – laboring
against sleep, agasp!)
                    – and does not waken.

Sees, alive (asleep)
            – the fall's roar entering
his sleep (to be fulfilled)
                              reborn
in his sleep – scattered over the mountain
severally

        – by which he woos her, severally.

And the amnesic crowd (the scattered),
called about – strains
to catch the movement of one voice

                                    hears,
              Pleasure! Pleasure!

                                        – feels,
half dismayed, the afternoon of complex
voices its own –
                    and is relieved
                            (relived)

        A cop is directing traffic
        across the main road up
        a little wooded slope toward
        the conveniences:

                        oaks, choke-cherry,
dogwoods, white and green, iron-wood   :
humped roots matted into the shallow soil
– mostly gone: rock out-croppings
polished by the feet of the picnickers:
sweetbarked sassafras   .

leaning from the rancid grease:
                                    deformity –

– to be deciphered (a horn, a trumpet!)
an elucidation by multiplicity,
a corrosion, a parasitic curd, a clarion
for belief, to be good dogs   :

NO DOGS ALLOWED AT LARGE IN THIS PARK

                    *   *   *

The descent beckons
            as the ascent beckoned
                        Memory is a kind
of accomplishment
            a sort of renewal
                        even
an initiation, since the spaces it opens are new

places
            inhabited by hordes
                        heretofore unrealized,
of new kinds –
            since their movements
                        are towards new objectives
(even though formerly they were abandoned)

No defeat is made up entirely of defeat – since
the world it opens is always a place
                        formerly
                                    unsuspected. A
world lost,
            a world unsuspected
                        beckons to new places
and no whiteness (lost) is so white as the memory
of whiteness   .

With evening, love wakens
            though its shadows
                        which are alive by reason
of the sun shining –
            grow sleepy now and drop away
                        from desire   .
Love without shadows stirs now
            beginning to waken
                        as night
advances.

The descent
            made up of despairs
                        and without accomplishment
realizes a new awakening   :
                        which is a reversal
of despair.

For what we cannot accomplish, what
is denied to love,
          what we have lost in the anticipation –
                              a descent follows,
endless and indestructible   .

* * *

On this most voluptuous night of the year
the term of the moon is yellow with no light
the air's soft, the night bird has
only one note, the cherry tree in bloom

makes a blur on the woods, its perfume
no more than half guessed moves in the mind.
No insect is yet awake, leaves are few.
In the arching trees there is no sleep.

The blood is still and indifferent, the face
does not ache nor sweat soil nor the
mouth thirst. Now love might enjoy its play
and nothing disturb the full octave of its run.

FROM BOOK THREE

THE LIBRARY

i

I love the locust tree
the sweet white locust
          How much?
          How much?
How much does it cost
to love the locust tree
          in bloom?

A fortune bigger than
Avery could muster
    So much
    So much
the shelving green
    locust
whose bright small leaves
    in June
lean among flowers
sweet and white at
    heavy cost

                  A cool of books
will sometimes lead the mind to libraries
of a hot afternoon, if books can be found
cool to the sense to lead the mind away.

For there is a wind or ghost of a wind
in all books echoing the life
there, a high wind that fills the tubes
of the ear until we think we hear a wind,
actual   .

                  to lead the mind away.

Drawn from the streets we break off
our minds' seclusion and are taken up by
the books' winds, seeking, seeking
down the wind
until we are unaware which is the wind and
which the wind's power over us
                to lead the mind away

and there grows in the mind
a scent, it may be, of locust blossoms
whose perfume is itself a wind moving
                to lead the mind away

through which, below the cataract
soon to be dry
the river whirls and eddies
                              first recollected.

Spent from wandering the useless
streets these months, faces folded against
him like clover at nightfall, something
has brought him back to his own
                              mind   .

                    in which a falls unseen
tumbles and rights itself
and refalls – and does not cease, falling
and refalling with a roar, a reverberation
not of the falls but of its rumor
                              unabated

                              Beautiful thing,
my dove, unable and all who are windblown,
touched by the fire
                    and unable,
a roar that (soundless) drowns the sense
with its reiteration
                    unwilling to lie in its bed
and sleep and sleep, sleep
                    in its dark bed.

Summer! it is summer   .
– and still the roar in his mind is
unabated

FROM BOOK FOUR

What's that?
– a duck, a hell-diver? A swimming dog?
What, a sea-dog? There it is again.
A porpoise, of course, following
the mackerel . No. Must be the up-
end of something sunk. But this is moving!
Maybe not. Flotsam of some sort.

A large, compact bitch gets up, black,
from where she has been lying
under the bank, yawns and stretches with
a half suppressed half whine, half cry
She looks to sea, cocking her ears and,
restless, walks to the water's edge where
she sits down, half in the water .

When he came out, lifting his knees
through the waves she went to him frisking
her rump awkwardly
Wiping his face with his hand he turned
to look back to the waves, then
knocking at his ears, walked up
to stretch out flat on his back in
the hot sand .   there were some
girls, far down the beach, playing ball.

– must have slept. Got up again, rubbed
the dry sand off and walking a
few steps got into a pair of faded
overalls, slid his shirt on overhand (the
sleeves were still rolled up) shoes,
hat where she had been watching them under

the bank and turned again
to the water's steady roar, as of a distant
waterfall   .   Climbing the
bank, after a few tries, he picked
some beach plums from a low bush and
sampled one of them, spitting the seed out,
then headed inland, followed by the dog

FROM BOOK FIVE

A flight of birds, all together,
seeking their nests in the season
a flock before dawn, small birds
'That slepen al the night with open ye,'
moved by desire, passionately, they
have come a long way, commonly.
Now they separate and go by pairs
each to his appointed mating. The
colors of their plumage are undecipherable
in the sun's glare against the sky
but the old man's mind is stirred
by the white, the yellow, the black
as if he could see them there.

Their presence in the air again
calms him. Though he is approaching
death he is possessed by many poems.
Flowers have always been his friends,
even in paintings and tapestries
which have lain through the past
in museums jealously guarded, treated
against moths. They draw him imperiously
to witness them, make him think
of bus schedules and how to avoid
the irreverent – to refresh himself
at the sight direct from the 12th

century what the old women or the young
or men or boys wielding their needles
to put in her green thread correctly
beside the purple, myrtle beside
holly and the brown threads beside:
together as the cartoon has plotted it
for them. All together, working together –
all the birds together. The birds
and leaves are designed to be woven
in his mind eating and   .   .
all together for his purposes

INDEX OF TITLES

INDEX OF TITLES

INDEX OF FIRST LINES